BRING
COLOUR
TO
CROCHET

64 multi-coloured squares

BRING COLOUR TO CROCHET

64 multi-coloured squares

RENATE KIRKPATRICK

SALLYMILNER
PUBLISHING

First published in 2010 by
Sally Milner Publishing Pty Ltd
734 Woodville Road
Binda NSW 2583 AUSTRALIA

© Renate Kirkpatrick 2010

Design: Anna Warren, Warren Ventures Pty Ltd
Editing: Anne Savage
Photography: Tim Connolly

Printed in China

National Library of Australia Cataloguing-in-Publication entry

Author:	Kirkpatrick, Renate, 1951-
Title:	Bring colour to crochet : 64 multi coloured squares / Renate Kirkpatrick.
ISBN:	9781863514149 (pbk.)
Series:	Milner craft series.
Subjects:	Crocheting--Patterns.
	Color in art.
Dewey Number:	746.434041

Disclaimer
Information and instructions given in this book are presented in good faith, but no warranty is given nor results guaranteed, nor is freedom from any patent to be inferred. As we have no control over physical conditions surrounding application of information herein contained in this book, the author and publisher disclaim any liability for untoward results.

10 9 8 7 6 5 4 3 2

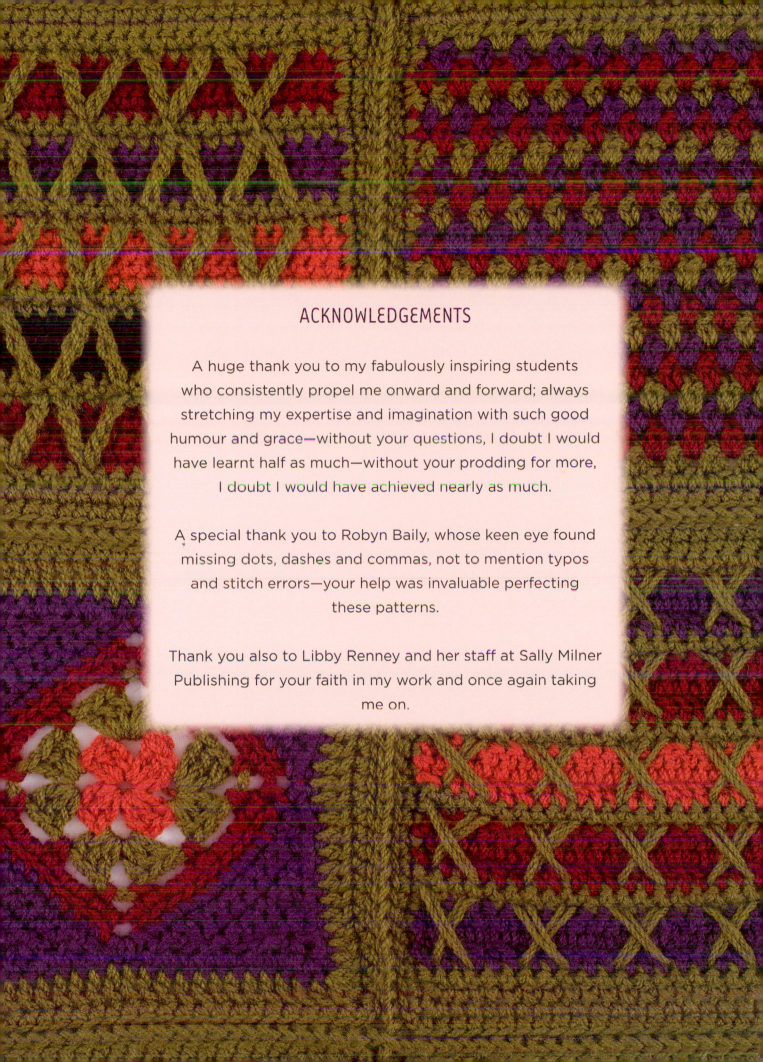

ACKNOWLEDGEMENTS

A huge thank you to my fabulously inspiring students who consistently propel me onward and forward; always stretching my expertise and imagination with such good humour and grace—without your questions, I doubt I would have learnt half as much—without your prodding for more, I doubt I would have achieved nearly as much.

A special thank you to Robyn Baily, whose keen eye found missing dots, dashes and commas, not to mention typos and stitch errors—your help was invaluable perfecting these patterns.

Thank you also to Libby Renney and her staff at Sally Milner Publishing for your faith in my work and once again taking me on.

Requirements for 64-pattern sampler in photo:

Bendigo Woollen Mills Classic 8-Ply yarn (100% pure wool)

Col A: 1200 g Sequoia (green)

Col B: 300 g Cranberry (red)

Col C: 250 g Burnt Orange (orange)

Col D: 250 g Plum (purple)

Col E: 200 g Ink (navy)

THE COMPLETED SAMPLER RUG

THE AIM OF THIS BOOK

The aim of this book is to present the reader with 64 interesting and practical stitch patterns that explore the many varied ways of incorporating colour and novelty into their work. Bringing colour into a project can be as easy as working rows of surface chains across some plain double crochet—dc (US sc) to more challenging techniques as changing colour within a given pattern. Freeformers too, will discover some novel stitches and interesting ways of bringing colour to their work.

DEDICATION

To all crochet diehards—your endless interest and enthusiasm keeps this wonderful craft alive and kicking.

Contents

Introduction: why another sampler rug?

I have always been a great advocate of the sampler rug. Aside from being an excellent teaching tool, the project itself becomes a practical goal-setter. As with previous samplers, *Bring Colour to Crochet* is a collection of stitch patterns ranging from the familiar for the less experienced, to the challenging for the more experienced. Utilising all 64 pattern squares will result in a rug approximately 152 cm (60 inches) square, but there is no reason why you can't choose a selection of favourites (say 30 to 36 squares) for a smaller knee rug—either way, by working your way through the assortment of stitch patterns you are not only increasing your crochet repertoire and inadvertently gathering confidence but you also achieve that wonderful feeling of satisfaction that comes with the accomplishment of a job well done—a functional rug to show off to one and all, a beautiful heirloom that can be proudly passed down the generations.

Crochet fundamentals

I've included the following crochet fundamentals to refresh the memory and help you on your way of bringing colour into your work—enjoy.

Bits and pieces you'll need

- A collection of yarn for swatches to try out unfamiliar stitches
- Blunt darning needle for sewing in tail ends
- Scissors
- Rust-proof pins
- Safety pins, markers, short lengths of yarn (for markers)
- Tape measure

Reading patterns

Sometimes crochet patterns can be rather wordy, particularly circular motifs that require instruction for each round—this can be a daunting experience, especially for the beginner. My advice is to glance through the pattern and see if there's anything unusual that you need to know, then go back to the beginning and follow the pattern from one comma to the next comma. Everything between those commas is one instruction. For example: 1 ch, dc (US sc) in next 3 sts, means 'make the 1 ch, then work a dc (US sc) in each of the next 3 stitches', and so on.

Don't be frightened by the terminology and symbols; you'll soon be familiar with what, to the newcomer, looks like another language. Above all, take your time. If you come across a particularly complicated section and you're having trouble nutting it out, put your work aside for the minute, make yourself a cup of tea and take a deep breath. Then, have another go—you'll often find it's not nearly as complicated as you first thought.

And I strongly suggest making use of both the written patterns and diagrams. You will be surprised how much clearer the instructions become.

Markers

In the past I considered markers a needless interruption to the job at hand and rarely used them. Then a particularly complicated project came along where markers were essential, and I suddenly realised how helpful they really are. The small amount of time it takes to place them saves hours in the long run and I have used them ever since. I use markers to indicate right side or top/bottom of work, first stitch of round, centre stitches in corners— and my crocheting life has never been easier. Commercial markers can be purchased from any craft supplier but safety pins or short yarn off-cuts (which I use) do the job just as well.

Yarn

My advice is always to use yarn you like working with (but preferably in the same ply as the pattern recommends). I'm not a purist and never shy away from using economy yarn if a colour or texture (or both, if you're lucky) is right for a particular project. Later, when you've gained experience and grown in confidence, you may decide to spend a little more on your yarn. Remember to purchase enough of the dye lot to complete your project. It's always better to have a little too much than running out with two motifs to go. It's also a good idea to keep yarn labels as reference so that if a dye lot has run out where you purchased it, you can, if need be, contact the manufacturer.

Swatches

Being usually in too much of a hurry getting on with the project in hand, I've never really been a great advocate of making swatches (unless it's a garment where size is an issue). However, this book does include a couple of tricky patterns that would benefit from being worked out beforehand using some scrap yarn, and thereby saving wear and tear on the better yarn I presume you would be working with.

Tension and dimension

The rug dimensions given earlier are only a guide; how loosely or tightly you crochet, and the size hook you use, will all influence the dimensions of your rug, but the few centimetres difference that may result overall aren't vital. The hook size and yarns given are recommendations only and by no means have to be complied with. It's far more important that your work is consistent, something that is much easier to achieve if you're working in your own comfort zone. This is your project; work with the hook size, colours and yarns you prefer. Enjoyment, knowledge and confidence are the aim—not trying to reproduce the exact same rug, either in size or colour, as mine.

A helpful tip for keeping yarn flowing freely is taking it from the centre of the ball. This way the yarn comes to you and not the other way round.

Determining square size

From time to time, fold your square corner to corner to determine how many rows you require before the top corners meet. When coming to the end of the square, try ending with the row most similar to the first row. For example, if the first row was worked in dc (US sc), then finish on a row of dc (US sc).

Edging

When edging your squares/motifs it is imperative that you work the number of stitches stated in the pattern (three stitches in corners and a certain number of stitches between). The top and bottom edges are usually straightforward, utilising the first and last row stitches as required. It's the two side edges that sometimes pose a bit of a problem because there are no obvious stitches to work. Nevertheless it's important that the same number of stitches is worked along these sides— even though you may feel that stitches are being squeezed in or too far apart. Just work as neatly and evenly as you can. The reason will become clear later when you join your squares (or motifs) stitch for stitch.

Tips for an attractive finish

It would be a real shame after spending many diligent hours working out the patterns only to have your project spoiled by an unsightly overall finish.

In my experience the most common mistakes made in crochet are at the beginning and end of rows due to the confusion as to where to work the first and last stitch. If your work has uneven edges that zigzag here and there, or leans off to one side, there's a good chance this fundamental is being overlooked. I hope the following Guide to Crochet Stitches and Techniques will help remedy this frustrating dilemma.

Guide to crochet stitches and techniques

The *foundation chain* is the number of chains required for the length and/or pattern plus the extra chains that are required to accommodate the height of stitch in the row about to be worked. For example: if trebles (US double crochet) are being used you will need 2 extra chains for the foundation chain and 3 extra chains on each working row.

These 3 extra chains are called the *turning chain*, and (unless the pattern states otherwise) must always counted as the *first stitch* of the row or round. Therefore, in subsequent rows or rounds, the turning chain must be treated as a stitch at the end of each previous row or round.

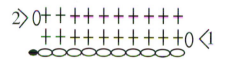

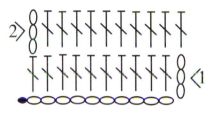

Stitch in use/abbrev.	Turning ch	Work 1st stitch on foundation ch
(US term/abbrev.)		
Double crochet—dc (US single crochet—sc)	1 ch	2nd ch from hook
Half treble—htr (US half double crochet—hdc)	2 ch	3rd ch from hook
Treble—tr (US double crochet—dc)	3 ch	4th ch from hook
Double treble—dtr (US treble—tr)	4 ch	5th ch from hook
Triple treble—ttr (US double treble—dtr)	5 ch	6th ch from hook
Quadruple treble—qtr (US double treble—trtr)	6 ch	7th ch from hook

Where to work the first stitch?

For double crochet (US single crochet)/ dc (US sc), insert hook in first stitch to start new row:

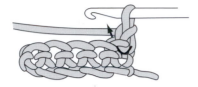

For all tall posted stitches, insert hook in second stitch to start new row. The example shows trebles (US double crochet)/tr (US dc):

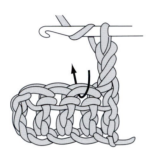

Changing colour, bringing in new yarn and tail-ends

Due the nature of this project you will be changing colour often and therefore producing lots of tail-ends. This brings us to another common problem—the false economy of leaving short tail-ends. Leave reasonable length tail-ends that can be easily and securely woven in later with a blunt darning needle—nothing spoils your work more than fluffy ends popping up. Better still, wherever possible crochet over the ends as you work—it saves on that big job at the end. And, when joining new yarn, avoid using knots. They produce weak spots

and have the annoying habit of moving to the front of your work.

The following two methods are the standard recommendations as the neatest ways of bringing in new yarn, and apply whether changing colour or just bringing in new yarn as the current ball runs out.

- Working with one colour: place new yarn along the top of your work and crochet a few stitches over it before the old yarn runs out; then pick up the new and crochet over the old.
- Working with two colours: when 2 loops of last stitch remain on hook, drop old colour, pick up new colour and draw through 2 loops.

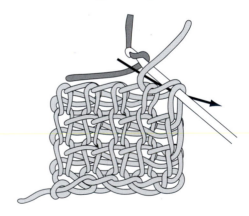

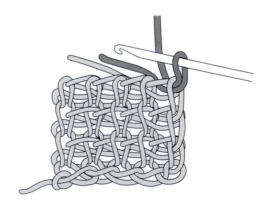

Bringing in Colour also introduces you to three novel ways of changing colour throughout your work which are explained further in the appropriate stitch patterns:

- Surface embellishing with chain stitch.
- Picking up the new colour from row or rows below before turning work.
- Not turning your work and bringing in the new colour at the beginning of the same row.

Blocking

As a general rule, I do not block sampler squares or motifs unless I feel it's absolutely necessary. As your pile of squares begins to grow, many of you may become concerned by their slight variations in size and feel the need to block them to size. This variation is due to the variety of stitch patterns used in each one, and blocking is certainly one way of bringing them into line. However, and I can't stress this enough (you have to trust me here), if the correct number of stitches have been worked around the edge, this will not be a problem, and blocking becomes an unnecessary exercise. Later you will be joining the squares stitch for stitch, which naturally brings them together. I also advise draping the finished rug over a lounge for a week or so and letting it drop into shape. If by chance you find a square exceedingly out of line with the rest, it may be worth making it again using a smaller or larger hook depending on what's required.

Methods for those who want to block:

1. Place square on a terry towel over a flat surface and, using rustproof pins, secure each square to shape, lightly steam and allow to dry completely. Be aware that the heat and steam can weaken the body fibre of some yarns and flatten textured stitches.

2. I prefer this second method for the least amount of interference to the yarn's body fibre and for retaining textured stitches: secure squares as for the first method, then liberally apply spray starch and allow to dry completely.

Using the placement chart

This placement chart is a guide only. Where different colours have been used, you may have to move the squares around to achieve the most pleasing colour arrangement.

Zigzag 16	Ripple 29	Variable Stripes 55	Bricks and Boxes 62	Shells 14	Variable Stripes 53 →	Shells 15	Variable Stripes 52 →
Ripple 30	Bricks and Boxes 63	Afghan 48	Clusters and Bobbles 43	Novelty 56	Zigzag 18	Bricks and Boxes 61	Novelty 57
Zigzag 20	Clusters and Bobbles 45	Relief 22	Afghan 49	Relief 23	Mosaic 39	Basic Stripe 1 →	Spike 7
Ripple 26	Mosaic 40	Chains 33	Chains 32	Afghan 46	Spike 10	Relief 24	Relief 21
Basic Stripe 4 →	Clusters and Bobbles 42	Novelty 58	Novelty 59	Chains 34	Afghan 47	Basic Stripe 2 →	Zigzag 17
Shells 13	Basic Stripe 3 →	Basic Stripe 5	Spike 6	Novelty 60	Spike 9	Afghan 50	Ripple 27
Variable Stripes 51 →	Shells 11	Mosaic 37	Ripple 28	Variable Stripes 54 →	Mosaic 38	Zigzag 19	Relief 25
Mosaic 36	Chains 35	Chains 31	Clusters and Bobbles 44	Spike 8	Clusters and Bobbles 41	Shells 12	Bricks and Boxes 64

Note: the horizontal arrows indicate squares that have been turned on their sides for variation.

Joining individual squares

Lay out squares according to the placement chart or as desired, and pin them together. For easier handling, work with just two rows at a time. Take care to always join the rows from the same end.

Working from right to left, with right sides of both squares facing up, work back loop (centre loops) of both squares, join in first sts using one of the joining techniques listed below:

1. **Invisible join using mattress stitch (ladder st):** with right side facing, lay square or motif to be joined side-by-side on a flat surface and with a blunt ended darning needle join in back loop of one square/motif:
   - slide the needle through two loops of second square/motif then two loops of the first again
   - repeat a couple of times and draw together firmly
   - manually ease the stitches back gently with your fingers
   - continue until the join is complete.
   - weave in ends

2. **Visible or flat join using whip stitch:** with the wrong sides of square/motif facing and using a blunt ended darning needle overcast stitch each corresponding st together to end. Weave in ends.

3. **Slip stitch join:** join with ss in first sts and ss each corresponding st together to end. Weave in ends.

4. **Double crochet (US single crochet) join:** join with dc (US sc) in first sts, dc (US sc) each corresponding st together to end. Weave in ends. This method, which is the strongest, was used for the sampler in photo.

Note: with dc (US sc) method, start with slip knot on hook, insert hook into st or sp indicated and draw up a loop, YO and draw through both loops on hook—counts as first dc (US sc)

All-round border edging (when all squares are joined)

Round 1: (work in back loops only) with right side facing, join Col A with dc in back loop of any corner st, work 2 dc in same st, *dc in each st to next corner st, 3 dc in corner st, repeat from * around join with ss to first dc, do not finish off.

Round 2: (work in both loops) cont with Col A, 1 ch, *dc in same st and in each st across to next corner st, 3 dc in next corner st, repeat from * around, join with ss to first dc, finish off.

Round 3: (work in both loops; for picot st see below) join Col E with dc in any corner st, 2 dc in same st and in next st (dc, picot st, dc) in next corner st, *work 5 dc, 1 picot st, 5 dc across to next corner st, (1 dc, 1 picot st, 1 dc) in corner st, repeat from * around, join with ss to first dc—finish off.

Picot stitch: make 1 dc in next st, 3 ch, then ss in 3rd ch from hook—picot made.

Stitch guide: basic crochet stitches

Abbreviations

ch	chain
ss	slip stitch
dc (US sc)	double crochet (US single crochet)
ldc (US Lsc	long double crochet (US long single crochet)
htr (US hdc)	half treble (US half double crochet)
tr (US dc)	treble (US double crochet)
ltr (US Ldc)	long treble (US long double crochet
dtr (US tr)	double treble (US treble)
ttr (US dtr)	triple treble (US double treble)
FP	front post
BP	back post
YO	yarn over

The following are standard stitch guides—variations are explained further in individual patterns where required.

SLIP KNOT

Use slip knots rather than just tying an ordinary knot—it's neater and allows the next chain (ch 1) to flow rather than being tugged through the loop just made. Never count the loop (on hook) as a chain or stitch.

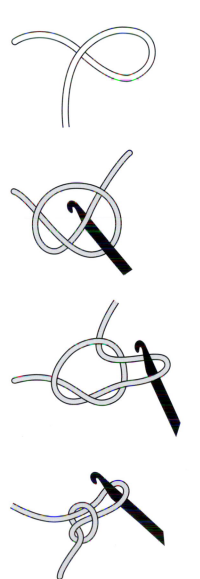

FOUNDATION CHAIN: CHAIN/CH

The number of chains required for length and/or pattern plus the extra chains that are required to accommodate the stitch height.

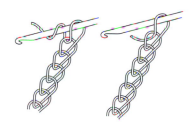

SLIP STITCH/SS

Insert hook into st, YO and draw yarn through st and loop on hook.

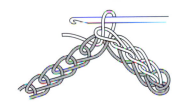

DOUBLE CROCHET/DC
(US SINGLE CROCHET/SC)

Working along foundation ch, insert hook into 2nd ch from hook, YO and draw loop through st (2 loops on hook), YO and draw yarn through both loops—dc (US sc) made.

HALF TREBLE/HTR (US HALF DOUBLE CROCHET/HDC)

Working along foundation ch, YO, insert hook into 3rd ch from hook, YO and draw loop through st (3 loops on hook), YO and draw yarn through all three loops—htr (US hdc) made.

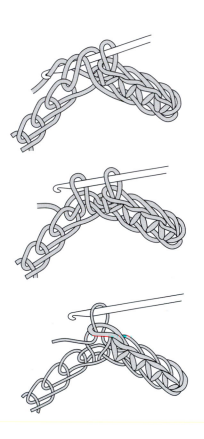

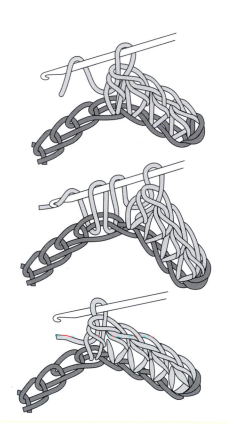

TREBLE/TR (US DOUBLE CROCHET/DC)

Working along foundation ch, YO, insert hook into 4th ch from hook, YO and draw yarn through st (3 loops on hook), YO, draw through 2 loops, YO and draw through last 2 loops—tr (US dc) made.

DOUBLE TREBLE/DTR (US TREBLE CROCHET/TR)

YO twice, Insert hook in st or sp and pull up a loop, YO and draw through 2 loops on hook 3 times.

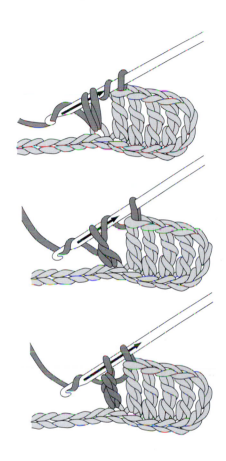

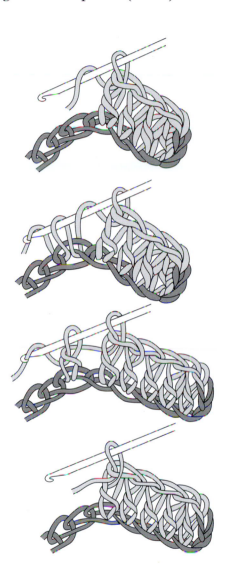

FRONT OR BACK LOOP ONLY

Work only in loop indicated by arrow.

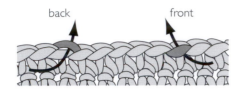

POST STITCH (FP OR BP)

Work around post of stitch indicated in row or rows below, inserting hook in direction of arrow.

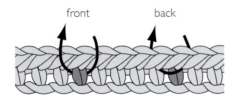

BEGINNING CLUSTER

3ch, (YO, insert hook in ring and pull up a loop, YO and draw through 2 loops on hook) twice, YO and draw through all 3 loops on hook.

CLUSTER

YO, insert hook in stitch or space and pull up a loop, YO and draw through 2 loops on hook) 3 times, YO and draw through all 4 loops on hook.

POPCORN

Work 5 tr or htr in st or sp, drop loop from hook, insert hook in first st of group, hook dropped loop and draw through, 1ch to close.

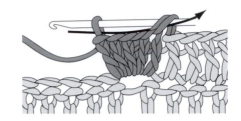

PUFF STITCH

(YO, insert hook in st or space, YO and pull up a loop even with hook) 3 or 4 times, YO and draw through all 7 or 9 loops on hook, 1 ch to close.

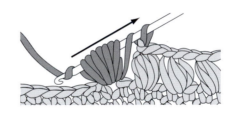

FINISHING OFF (CASTING OFF STITCH)

With the last stitch complete, cut yarn, and draw though the loop on hook, pull tight to close the loop. Weave in end. With slippery yarn, draw through the loop twice (make an extra chain) and pull down very tightly with your thumb to close. Weave in end.

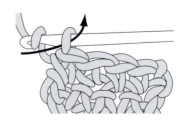

BRINGING IN COLOUR DIAGRAM SYMBOLS

- = slip stitch (sl st)
- = chain (ch)
- = double crochet (dc)
- = half treble (htr)
- = treble (tr)
- = double treble (dtr)
- = triple treble (ttr)

= work in front loop
a   b   c

= work in back loop
a   b   c   d

= front post
a   b   c   d   e   f   g   h   i   j

= back post
a   b   c   d   e   f   g   h   i   j

= decrease
a   b   c

= spike st
a   b   c   d   e   f

= reverse dc (crab st)

= reverse dc (crab st) in front loop

= fasten off

= bring in new yarn or colour

= unused loop

< > = row

= puff
a   b

= beg cluster
a   b   c

= cluster
a   b   c   d   e   f   g

= beg popcorn

= popcorns
a   b   c

= wrap or offset st
a   b

= bullion with number of wraps

= bent bullion with number of wraps

= coil st

= spiral stitch

= twisted cable

EDGING FOR INDIVIDUAL SQUARES

I recommend that as you complete each square according to the instructions you then finish it with these two rounds of edging; if you don't edge as you go, you will end up with a pile of 64 squares to be done one after the other—a very tedious chore.

Round 1: (with right side facing) join Col A with dc (US sc) in any corner st, 1 ch, work 2 dc (US sc) in same corner st, *work 23 dc (US sc) evenly spaced to next corner st, 3 dc (US sc) in corner, repeat from * around square, join with ss in first dc (US sc), do not finish off—104 dc (US sc).

Round 2: cont with Col A, ch 1, dc (US sc) in same st and in each st across to next corner st, *3 dc (US sc) in corner st, dc (US sc) in each st across to next corner st, repeat from * around square, join with ss in first dc (US sc)—112 dc (US sc).

SIXTY-FOUR MULTI-COLOURED SQUARES

BASIC STRIPES

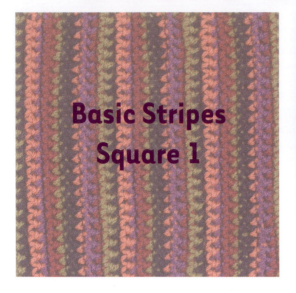

Basic Stripes
Square 1

Colours A, B, C, D and E are required for this pattern.

With col A make 26 ch.

Row 1: cont with col A, dc (US sc) in 2nd ch from hook and in each ch across to last 2 loops of last st, bringing in col E in last 2 loops to complete st, drop col A—25 dc (US sc).

Row 2: (right side) cont with col E, 1 ch, turn, dc (US sc) in each st across to last 2 loops of last st, bringing in col C in last 2 loops to complete st, drop col E—25 dc (US sc).

Row 3: repeat row 2 with col C, changing to col D.

Row 4: repeat row 2 with col D, changing to col B.

Row 5: repeat row 2 with col B, changing to col A.

Subsequent rows: repeat row 2, alternating colours as above (E-C-D-B-A).

Last row: repeat row 2 with col A, finish off.

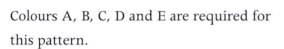

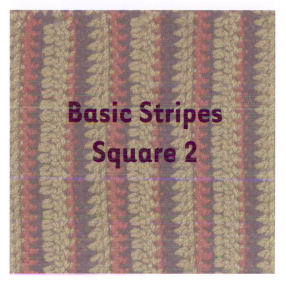

Basic Stripes Square 2

Colours A, B and E are required for this pattern.

With col A make 27 ch.

Row 1: (right side) cont with col A, tr (US dc) into 4th ch from hook and in each ch across to last 2 loops of last st, bringing in col B to complete last st, drop col A—25 tr (US dc).

Row 2: cont with col B, 1 ch, turn, dc (US sc) in first and in each st across to last 2 loops of last st, bringing in col E in last 2 loops to complete st, drop col B—25 dc (US sc).

Row 3: cont with col E, repeat row 2 to last 2 loops of last st, bringing in col A in last 2 loops to complete st, drop col E—25 dc (US sc).

Row 4: cont with col A, 3 ch (count as tr [US dc]), turn, tr (US dc) in next and in each st across to last 2 loops of last st, bringing in col B in last 2 loops to complete st, drop col A—25 tr (US dc).

Subsequent rows: repeat rows 2 to 4, alternating colours as above (A-B-E-A) ending with row 4, col A, and a last row as follows.

Last row: cont with col A, 1 ch, turn, dc (US sc) in first and in each st across, finish off.

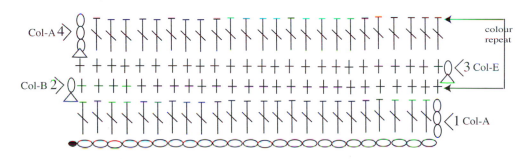

Basic Stripes Square 3

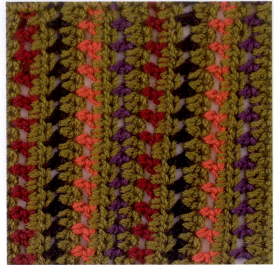

Colours A, B, C, D and E are required for this pattern.

With col A make 26 ch.

Row 1: (right side) cont with col A, htr (US hdc) in 3rd ch from hook and in each ch across to last 3 loops of last st, bringing in col B in last 3 loops to complete last st, drop col A—25 htr (US hdc).

Row 2: cont with col B, 3 ch (counts as htr [US hdc] + 1-ch sp), turn, *skip next st, htr (US hdc) in next st, 1 ch, repeat from * across, finish off col B—13 htr (US hdc) + 12 x 1-ch sps.

Row 3: do not turn, remove hook, reinsert hook into 2nd ch of beginning ch of same row and bring in col A, 2 ch (count as htr [US hdc]), htr (US hdc) into each st and 1-ch sp across to last 3 loops of last st, bringing in col E in last 3 loops to complete last st, drop col A—25 htr (US hdc).

Row 4: cont with col E, repeat row 2, changing to col A.

Row 5: cont with col A, repeat row 3, changing to col C.

Row 6: cont with col C, repeat row 2, changing to col A.

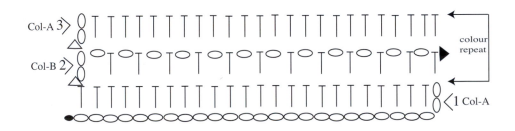

Row 7: cont with col A, repeat row 3, changing to col D.

Row 8: cont with col D, repeat row 2, changing to col A.

Subsequent rows: repeat rows 2 and 3, alternating colours as above (A-B-A-D-A-C-A-E), ending with row 3, col A.

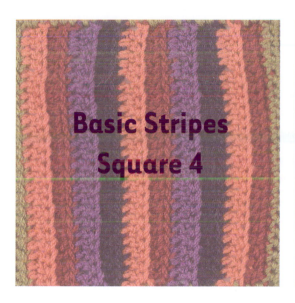

Colours A, B, C, D and E are required for this pattern.

With col A make 26 ch.

Row 1: (right side) cont with col A, dc (US sc) in 2nd ch from hook and in each ch across to last 2 loops of last st, bringing in col C in last 2 loops to complete st, finish off col A—25 dc (US sc).

Row 2: (work in front loops only) cont with col C, 3 ch (count as tr [US dc]), turn, tr (US dc) in next st and in each st across to last 2 loops of last st, bringing

in col B in last 2 loops to complete st, finish off col C—25 tr (US dc).

Row 3: (in back loops only) repeat row 2 with col B, changing to col D, finish off col B.

Row 4: (in front loops only) repeat row 2 with col D, changing to col E, finish off col D.

Row 5: (in back loops only) repeat row 2 with col E, changing to col A, finish off col E.

Subsequent rows: repeat row 2,

working in front or back loops as required and alternating colours as above (C-B-D-E) until square size reached, then bring in col A and work a last row as follows.

Last row: cont with col A, 1 ch, turn, dc (US sc) in first and in each st across, finish off—25 dc (US sc).

Work in front loops

Work in back loops

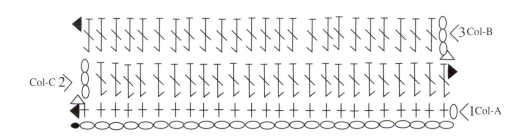

Basic Stripes Square 5

Colours A, B and E are required for this pattern.

With col A make 28 ch.

Row 1: (right side) cont with col A, dtr (US tr) in 5th ch from hook and in next

4 ch, tr (US dc) in next 6 ch, htr (US hdc) in next 6 ch, dc (US sc) in last 7 ch, bringing in col E in last 2 loops of last st to complete st, drop col A—25 sts.

Row 2: (in front loops only) cont with col E, 4 ch (count as dtr [US tr]), turn, dtr (US tr) in next 5 sts, tr (US dc) in next 6 sts, htr (US hdc) in next 6 sts, dc (US sc) in last 7 sts, bringing in col B in last 2 loops of last st to complete st, drop Col E—25 sts.

Row 3: (in back loops only) cont with col B, 4 ch, turn, dtr (US tr) in next 5 sts, tr (US dc) in next 6 sts, htr (US hdc) in next 6 sts, dc (US sc) in last 7 sts, bringing in col A in last 2 loops of last st to complete st, drop col B—25 sts.

Subsequent rows: repeat rows 2 and 3, alternating colours in the sequence A-E-B-A, ending with either row 2 or 3 in col A.

Work in front loops

Work in back loops

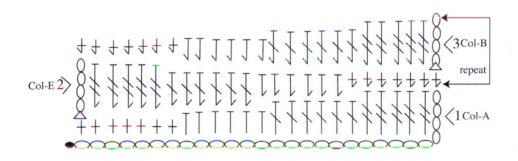

SPIKES

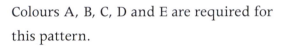

Spikes Square 6

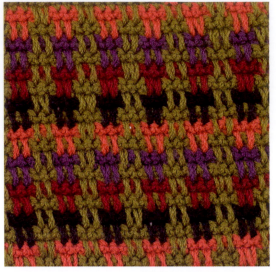

Colours A, B, C, D and E are required for this pattern.

With col A make 26 ch.

Row 1: (right side) cont with col A, dc (US sc) in 2nd ch from hook and in each ch across—25 dc (US sc).

Row 2: cont with col A, 1 ch, turn, dc (US sc) in first st and in each st across to last 2 loops of last st, bringing in Col C in last 2 loops to complete last st, drop col A—25 dc (US sc).

Row 3: cont with col C, 1 ch, turn, dc (US sc) in first 2 sts, *spike st in each next 2 sts directly 2 rows below, dc (US sc) in each next 2 sts, repeat from * across to last st, dc (US sc) in last st—12 spike sts.

Row 4: cont with col C, repeat row 2, changing to col A in last 2 loops of last st to complete st, finish off col C—25 dc (US sc).

Row 5: cont with col A, 1 ch, turn, *spike st in first 2 sts directly 2 rows below, dc (US sc) in next 2 sts, repeat from * across to last st, work last spike st directly 2 rows below as follows: work spike st as usual to last 2 loops on hook, insert hook into last dc (US sc) and draw up a loop, YO and draw through 3 loops on hook—13 spike sts.

Row 6: cont with col A, repeat row 2, changing to col E in last 2 loops of last st to complete st, drop col A—25 dc (US sc).

Subsequent rows: repeat rows 3 to 6, alternating colours in the sequence A-C-A-E-A-B-A-D-A, ending with row 2, col A.

Spike stitch: Insert hook into stitch indicated and draw up a long loop level with stitch on working row, YO and draw through 2 loops on hook—spike st made.

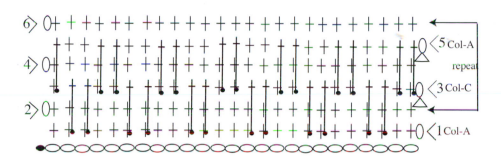

Spikes Square 7

Colours A, C and E are required for this pattern.

With col A make 26 ch.

Row 1: (right side) cont with col A, dc (US sc) in 2nd ch from hook and in each ch across—25 dc (US sc).

Row 2: cont with col A, 1 ch, turn, dc (US sc) in first and in each st across to last 2 loops of last st, bringing in col E in last 2 loops to complete st, drop col A—25 dc (US sc).

Row 3: cont with col E, 1 ch, turn, dc (US sc) in first st, *spike st in next st directly 2 rows below, dc (US sc) in next 3 st, repeat from * across—6 spike sts.

Row 4: cont with col E, repeat row 2, changing to col C in last 2 loops to complete st, drop col E—25 dc (US sc).

Row 5: cont with Col C, 1 ch, turn, dc (US sc) in first 2 sts, *spike st in next st directly 2 rows below, dc (US sc) in next 3 st, repeat from * across to last 2 sts, dc (US sc) in last 2 sts—6 spike sts.

Row 6: cont with col C, repeat row 2, changing to col A in last 2 loops of last st to complete st, drop col C—25 dc (US sc).

Row 7: cont with col A, 1 ch, turn, dc (US sc) in first 3 sts, *spike st in next st directly 2 rows below, dc (US sc) in next 3 st, repeat from * across to last st, dc (US sc) in last st—6 spike sts.

Row 8: cont with col A, repeat row 2, changing to Col E in last 2 loops of last st to complete st, drop col A—25 dc (US sc).

Row 9: cont with col E, 1 ch, turn, *spike st in first st directly 2 rows below, dc (US sc) in next 3 sts, repeat from * across to last st, spike st in last st directly 2 rows below, working last spike st as follows: work spike st as usual to last 2 loops on hook, insert hook into last st and draw up a loop, YO and draw through 3 loops on hook—7 spike sts.

Row 10: cont with col E, repeat row 2, changing to col C in last 2 loops of last st to complete st, drop col E—25 dc (US sc).

Subsequent rows: repeat rows 3 to 10, alternating colours in the sequence A-E-C-A, ending with row 2, col A.

Spike stitch: Insert hook into stitch indicated and draw up a long loop level with stitch on working row, YO and draw through 2 loops on hook—spike st made.

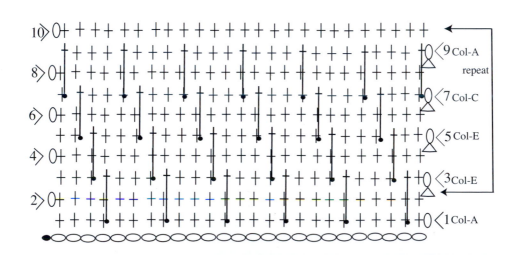

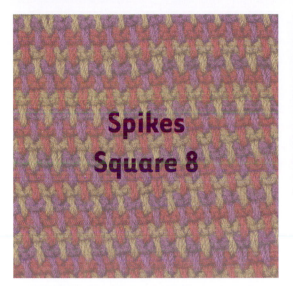

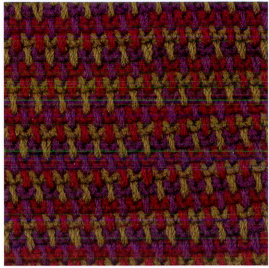

Colours A, B and D are required for this pattern.

With col A make 26 ch.

Row 1: (right side) cont with col A, dc (US sc) in 2nd ch from hook and in each ch across—25 dc (US sc).

Row 2: cont with col A, 1 ch, turn, dc (US sc) in first and in each st across to last 2 loops of last st, bringing in col B in last 2 loops to complete last st, drop col A—25 dc (US sc).

Row 3: cont with col B, 1 ch, turn, dc (US sc) in first st, *spike st in next st directly 2 rows below, dc (US sc) in next st, repeat from * across—12 spike sts.

Row 4: cont with col B, repeat row 2, changing to col D in last 2 loops to complete st, drop col B—25 dc (US sc).

Row 5: cont with col D, 1 ch, turn,

*spike st in first st directly 2 rows below, dc (US sc) in next st, repeat from * across to last st, spike st in last st directly 2 rows below, working last spike st as follows:

- work spike st as usual to last 2 loops on hook, insert hook into last st and draw up a loop, YO and draw through 3 loops on hook—13 spike sts.

Row 6: cont with col D, repeat row 2, changing to col A in last 2 loops of last st to complete st, drop col D—25 dc (US sc).

Subsequent rows: repeat rows 3 to 6, alternating colours in the sequence A-B-D-A, ending with row 2, col A.

Spike stitch: Insert hook into stitch indicated and draw up a long loop level with stitch on working row, YO and draw through 2 loops on hook—spike st made.

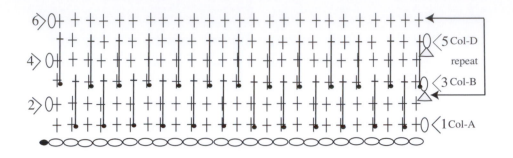

Spikes
Square 9

Colours A and D are required for this pattern.

With col A make 26 ch.

Row 1: cont with col A, dc (US sc) in 2nd ch from hook and in each ch across—25 dc (US sc).

Row 2: (right side) 1 ch, turn, dc (US sc) in first st and in each st across—25 dc (US sc).

Row3: cont with col A, 1 ch, turn, dc (US sc) in first st and in each st across to last 2 loops of last st, bringing in col D in last 2 loops to complete st, drop col A—25 dc (US sc).

Row 4: cont with col D, 1 ch, turn, dc (US sc) in first 2 sts, *work multi spike st 2 rows below, dc (US sc) in next 4 sts, repeat from * across to last 2 sts, dc (US sc) in last 2 sts—5 multi spike sts.

Rows 5 and 6: cont with col D, repeat row 2—25 dc (US sc).

Row 7: cont with col D, repeat row 3, changing to col A—25 dc (US sc).

Row 8: cont with col A, 1 ch, turn, dc (US sc) in first 5 sts, *work multi spike st 2 rows below, dc (US sc) in next 4 sts, repeat from * across—4 multi spike sts.

Rows 9 and 10: cont with col A, repeat row 2—25 dc (US sc).

Row 11: cont with col A, repeat row 3, changing to col D—25 dc (US sc).

Subsequent rows: repeat rows 4 to 11, ending with row 2, col A.

Spike stitch: Insert hook into stitch indicated and draw up a long loop level with stitch on working row, YO and draw through 2 loops on hook—spike st made.

Multi spike stitch: Working in row indicated, insert hook and draw up a loop, in dc (US sc) directly below dc (US sc) just made and in each next 2 dc (US sc) of same row, YO and draw through all 4 loops on hook—multi spike st made.

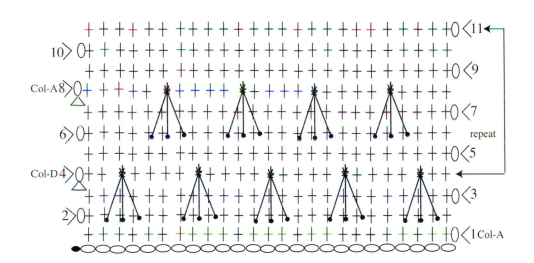

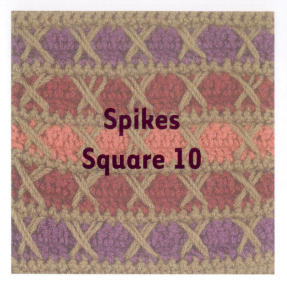

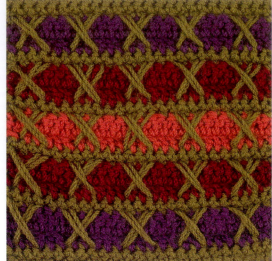

Colours A, B, C and D are required for this pattern.

With col A make 26 ch.

Row 1: (right side) cont with col A, dc (US sc) in 2nd ch from hook and in each ch across—25 dc (US sc).

Row 2: cont with col A, 1 ch, turn, dc (US sc) in first st, and in each st across to last 2 loops of last st, bringing in col D in last 2 loops of last st to complete st, drop col A—25 dc (US sc).

Row 3: cont with col D, 3 ch (count as tr), turn, tr next st and in each st across—25 tr.

Row 4: cont with col D, repeat row 3, bringing in col A in last 2 loops of last st to complete st, finish off col D—25 tr.

Row 5: skip unused tr behind spike st,

cont with col A, 1 ch, turn, dc (US sc) in first st, *work spike st in dc (US sc) 5 sts forward 3 rows below, dc (US sc) in next 2 sts on working row, work spike st in dc (US sc) 3 sts backward 3 rows below, dc (US sc) in next st on working row, repeat from * across to last 4 sts, work spike st in dc (US sc) 4 sts forward 3 rows below, dc (US sc) in next 2 sts on working row, working last spike st in dc (US sc) 3 sts backward 3 rows below as follows:

- work spike st as usual to last 2 loops on hook, insert hook into last st and draw up a loop, YO and draw through 3 loops on hook—5 x spike st crosses.

Row 6: cont col A, repeat row 2, changing to col B in last 2 loops of last st to complete st, drop col A—25 dc (US sc).

Subsequent rows: repeat rows 3 to 6, alternating colours in the sequence A-D-

A-B-A-C-A-B-A-D-A, ending with row 6, col A.

Spike stitch: Insert hook into stitch indicated and draw up a long loop level with stitch on working row, YO and draw through 2 loops on hook—spike st made.

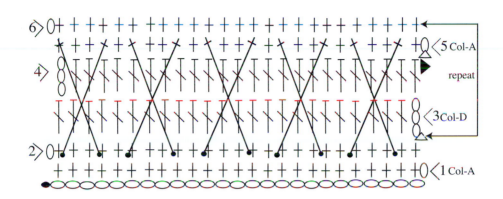

SHELLS

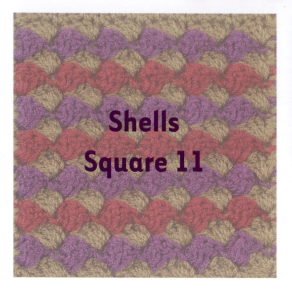

Colours A, B and D are required for this pattern.

With col A make 26 ch.

Row 1: (right side) cont with col A, dc (US sc) in 2nd ch from hook and in each ch across—25 dc (US sc).

Row 2: (wrong side) cont with col A, 1 ch, turn, *(dc [US sc], 3 tr [US dc]) in first st, skip 3 sts, repeat from * across to last st, dc (US sc) in last st, finish off col A—6 shells.

Row 3: (right side) turn work, remove hook and join col D with dc (US sc) in first st, 3 tr (US dc) in same st, skip next 3 sts, *(dc [US sc], 3 tr [US dc]) in next st, skip next 3 sts, repeat from * across to last st, dc (US sc) in last st, finish off col D—6 shells.

Row 4: (wrong side) turn work, remove hook and join col A with dc (US sc) in first st, 3 tr (US dc) in same st, skip next 3 sts, *(dc [US sc], 3 tr [US dc]) in next st, skip next 3 sts, repeat from * across to last st, dc (US sc) in last st, finish off—6 shells.

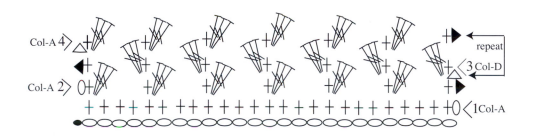

Subsequent rows: repeat rows 3 and 4, alternating colours in the sequence A-D-A-B, ending with row 4 in col A and a last row as follows.

Last row: cont with col A, 1 ch, turn, dc (US sc) in first st and in each st across, finish off—25 dc (US sc).

> **Joining with dc (US sc):** begin with a slip knot on hook. Insert hook into stitch or space indicated, YO and pull up loop, YO and draw through both loops on hook.

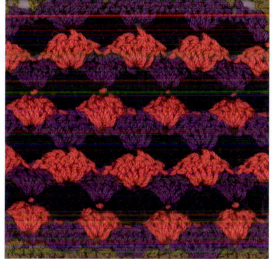

Colours A, C, D and E are required for this pattern.

With col A make 26 ch.

Row 1: (right side) cont with col A, dc (US sc) in 2nd ch from hook and in each ch across to last st, bring in col D in last 2 loops of last st to complete st, finish off col A—25 dc (US sc).

Row 2: cont with col D, 3 ch (count as tr [US dc]), turn, 2 tr (US dc) in same st, *skip 2 sts, dc (US sc) in next st, skip 2 sts, 5 tr (US dc) in next st, repeat from * across to last 3 sts, skip 2 sts, 3 tr (US dc) in last st, bringing in col C in last 2 loops of last st to complete st, drop col D—3 shells.

Row 3: cont with col C, 1 ch, turn, dc (US sc) in same st, *skip 2 sts, 5 tr (US dc) in next st, skip 2 sts, dc (US sc) in next st, repeat from * across to last 2 loops of last st, bringing in col E in last 2 loops to complete st, drop col C—4 shells.

Subsequent rows: repeat rows 2 and 3, alternating colours in the sequence D-C-E, then work 2 rows as follows.

2nd last row: bring in col A, 1 ch, turn, dc (US sc) in same st, *2 ch, skip next 2 sts, dc (US sc) in next st, repeat from * across, do not finish off—8 x 2-ch sps + 9 dc (US sc).

Last row: cont with col A, 1 ch, turn, dc (US sc) in same st, *2 dc (US sc) in next 2-ch sp, dc (US sc) in next st, repeat from * across, finish off—25 dc (US sc).

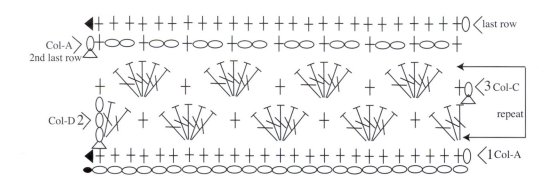

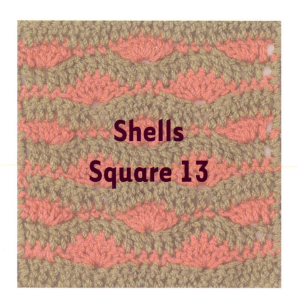

Shells Square 13

Colours A and C are required for this pattern.

With col A make 27 ch.

Row 1: (right side) cont with col A, tr (US dc) in 4th ch from hook and in each ch across, drop col A—25 tr (US dc).

Row 2: do not turn, remove hook, reinsert into top of beginning ch of same row and bring in col C, 1 ch, dc (US sc) in same st, dc (US sc) in next 3 sts, *skip next 3 sts, 7 dtr (US tr) in next st, skip next 3 sts, dc (US sc) in next 3 sts, repeat from * across, dc (US sc) in last st, bringing in col A in last 2 loops of last st to complete st, drop col C—2 shells.

Row3: Cont with col A, 3 ch (count as tr [US dc]), turn, tr (US dc) in next st and in each st across—25 tr (US dc).

Row 4: do not turn, remove hook, reinsert into top of beginning ch of same row and bring in col C, 3 ch, tr (US dc)

in next st, 4 dtr (US tr) in next st, *skip next 3 sts, dc (US sc) in next 3 sts, skip next 3 sts, 7 dtr (US tr) in next st, repeat from * across to last 3 sts, 4 dtr (US tr) in next st, tr (US dc) in each last 2 sts, bringing in Col A in last 2 loops of last st to complete st, drop col C—1 x shell + 2 x 4-tr (US dc) shells.

Row 5: cont with col, A repeat row 3—25 tr (US dc).

Subsequent rows: repeat rows 2 to 5, ending with row 5, col A, finish off.

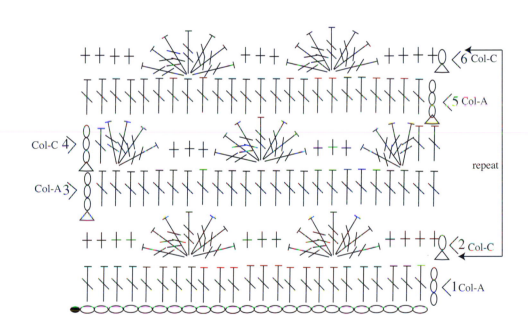

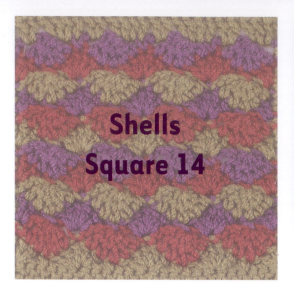

Colours A, B and D are required for this pattern.

With col A make 26 ch.

Row 1: cont with col A, dc (US sc) in 2nd ch from hook and in each ch across—25 dc (US sc).

Row 2: (right side) cont with col A, 3 ch (count as tr [US dc], beginning ch), turn, 2 tr (US dc) in same st, *skip next 2 sts, dc (US sc) in next st, skip next 2 sts, 5 tr (US dc) in next st, repeat from * across to last 3 sts, skip next 2 sts, 3 tr (US dc) in last st, bringing in col B in last 2 loops of last st to complete st, drop col A—3 x 5-tr (US dc) shells + 2 x 3-tr (US dc) shells.

Row 3: cont with col B, 1 ch, turn, dc (US sc) in same st, *2 ch, work cluster st over the next 5 sts, 2 ch, dc (US sc) in next st, repeat from * across, bringing in col D in last 2 loops of last st to complete st, drop Col B—4 x clusters + 8 x 2-ch sps.

Row 4: cont with col D, 3 ch, turn, 2 tr (US dc) in same st, *skip 2-ch sp, dc (US sc) in closing loop of next cluster st, skip 2-ch sp, 5 tr (US dc) in next st, repeat from * across to last 3 sts, skip next 2 sts, 3 tr (US dc) in last st, bringing in col A in last 2 loops of last st to complete st, drop col A—3 x 5-tr (US dc) shells + 2 x 3-tr (US dc) shells.

Row 5: cont with col A, repeat row 3, changing to col B.

Subsequent rows: repeat rows 4 and 5, alternating colours in the sequence A-B-D-A, ending with row 4, col D (changing to col A).

Last row: cont with col A, 3 ch, turn, *2 tr (US dc) in next 2-ch sp, tr (US dc) in closing loop of next cluster st, 2 tr (US dc) in next 2-ch sp, tr (US dc) in next st, repeat from * across—25 tr (US dc).

Cluster stitch: (YO, insert hook in st indicated and draw up a loop, YO and draw through 2 loops) repeat over number of sts indicated, YO and draw through all loops on hook, 1 ch to close—cluster st made.

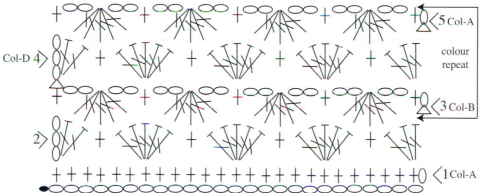

**Shells
Square 15**

Colours A, C and D are required for this pattern.

With col A make 26 ch.

This is a wide pattern; work tightly or use a smaller hook to stay in line with other 63 squares.

Row 1: (right side) cont with col A, dc (US sc) in 2nd ch from hook and in each ch across to last 2 loops of last st, bringing in col D in last 2 loops of last st to complete st, drop col A—25 dc (US sc).

Row 2: cont with col D, 3 ch (count as tr [US dc], beginning ch), turn, *work puff st in each next 2 sts, skip next 2 sts, 5 tr (US dc) in next st, skip next 2 sts, repeat from * across, tr (US dc) in last st, bringing in col C in last 2 loops of last st to complete st, drop col D—8 x puff sts + 3 x shells.

Row 3: cont with col C, 3 ch, turn, *work puff st in each next 2 puff sts, 5 tr (US dc) in next st, skip next 4 sts, repeat from * across, tr (US dc) in last st, bringing in col A in last 2 loops of last st to complete st, drop col C—8 x puff sts + 3 x shells.

Subsequent rows: repeat row 3, alternating colours in the sequence A-D-C, ending with a col C row, change to col A.

Last row: cont with col A, 2 ch, turn, *htr (US hdc) in next 2 puff sts, dc (US sc) in next 5 sts, repeat from * across, htr (US hdc) in last st—25 sts.

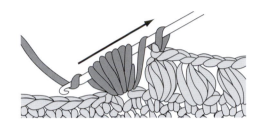

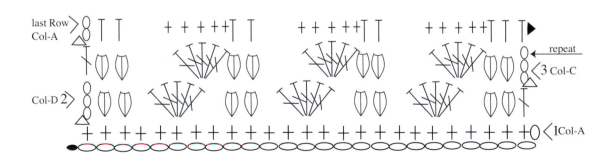

Puff stitch: (YO, insert hook in st indicated, YO and pull up a loop even with hook) 3 times, YO and draw through all 7 loops on hook, 1 ch to close—puff st made.

ZIGZAGS

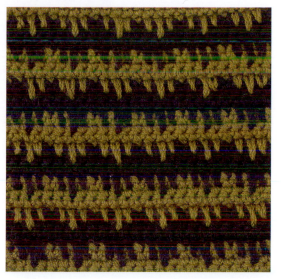

Colours A and E are required for this pattern.

With col A make 26 ch.

Row 1: cont with col A, dc (US sc) in 2nd ch from hook and in each ch across—25 dc (US sc).

Row 2: (right side) cont with col A, 1 ch, turn, dc (US sc) in first and in each st across—25 dc (US sc).

Row 3: cont with col A, 1 ch, turn, dc (US sc) in first and in each st across to last 2 loops of last st, bringing in col E in last 2 loops to complete last st, drop col A—25 dc (US sc).

Row 4: cont with col E, 1 ch, turn, dc (US sc) in first st, *spike st in next st directly 1 row below, spike st in next st directly 2 rows below, spike st in next st directly 1 row below, dc (US sc) in next st, repeat from * across—6 x 3-spike groups.

Rows 5 and 6: cont with col E, 1 ch, turn, dc (US sc) in first and in each st across—25 dc (US sc).

Row 7: cont with col E, 1 ch, turn, dc (US sc) in first and in each st across to last 2 loops of last st, bringing in col A in last 2 loops to complete last st, drop col E—25 dc (US sc).

Subsequent rows: repeat rows 4 to 7, alternating colours as required, ending with row 4, col A.

Spike stitch: Insert hook into stitch indicated and draw up a long loop level with stitch on working row, YO and draw through 2 loops on hook—spike st made.

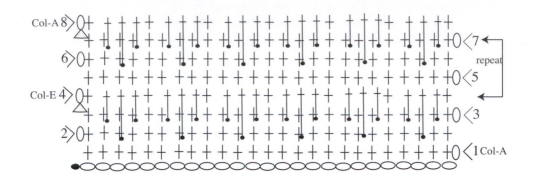

Zigzags
Square 17

Colours A and C are required for this pattern.

With col A make 26 ch.

Row 1: (right side) cont with col A, dc (US sc) in 2nd ch from hook and in each ch across—25 dc (US sc).

Rows 2 to 5: cont with col A, 1 ch, turn, dc (US sc) in first and in each st across—25 dc (US sc).

Row 6: cont with col A, 1 ch, turn, dc (US sc) in first and in each st across to last 2 loops of last st, bringing in col C in last 2 loops to complete st, finish off col A—25 dc (US sc).

Row 7: cont with col C, 1 ch, turn, dc (US sc) in first st, *spike st in next st directly 1 row below, spike st in next st directly 2 rows below, spike st in next st directly 3 rows below, spike st in next st directly 4 rows below, spike st in next st directly 5 rows below, dc (US sc) in next st, repeat from * across—4 x 5-spike groups.

Rows 8 to 11: cont with col C, 1 ch, turn, dc (US sc) in first and in each st across—25 dc (US sc).

Row 12: cont with col C, 1 ch, turn, dc (US sc) in first and in each st across to last 2 loops of last st, bringing in col A in last 2 loops to complete last st, finish off col C—25 dc (US sc).

Subsequent rows: repeat rows 7 to 12, alternating colours as required, ending with row 7, col C, finish off.

Spike stitch: Insert hook into stitch indicated and draw up a long loop level with stitch on working row, YO and draw through 2 loops on hook—spike st made.

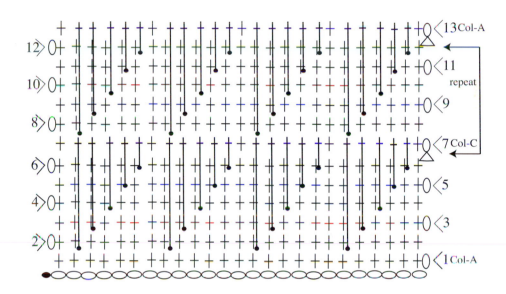

Zigzags
Square 18

Colours A and B are required for this pattern.

With col A make 26 ch.

Row 1: (right side) cont with col A, dc (US sc) in 2nd ch from hook and in each ch across to last 2 loops of last st, bringing in col B in last 2 loops to complete st, finish off col A—25 dc (US sc).

Rows 2 to 5: cont with col B, 1 ch, turn, dc (US sc) in first and in each st across—25 dc (US sc).

Row 6: cont with col B, 1 ch, turn, dc (US sc) in first and in each st across to last 2 loops of last st, bringing in col A to complete st, drop col B—25 dc (US sc).

Row 7: cont with col A, 1 ch, turn, dc (US sc) in first 2 sts, *spike st in next st

directly 1 row below, spike st in next st directly 2 rows below, spike st in next st directly 3 rows below, spike st in next st directly 4 rows below, spike st in next st directly 5 rows below, spike st in next st directly 4 rows below, spike st in next st directly 3 rows below, spike st in next st directly 2 rows below, spike st in next st directly 1 row below, dc (US sc) in next 3 sts, repeat from * across to last 2 sts, dc (US sc) in last 2 sts, finish off col A—2 x 9-spike groups.

Row 8: do not turn, remove hook, reinsert into first dc (US sc) of same row and bring in col B, 1 ch, dc (US sc) in first and in each st across—25 dc (US sc).

Rows 9 to 12: 1 ch, turn, dc (US sc) in first and in each st across—25 dc (US sc).

Row 13: cont with col B, 1 ch, turn, dc (US sc) in each st across to last 2 loops of last st, bringing in col A in last 2 loops

Subsequent rows: repeat rows 2 to 13, alternating colours as required, ending with row 7, col B, finish off—4 x 5-spike groups.

Spike stitch: Insert hook into stitch indicated and draw up a long loop level with stitch on working row, YO and draw through 2 loops on hook—spike st made.

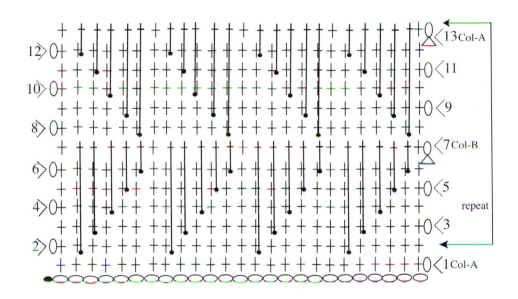

Reliefs
Square 22

Colours A and D are required for this pattern.

With col A make 27 ch.

Row 1: (right side) cont with col A, tr in 4th ch from hook and in each ch across—25 tr.

Row 2: cont with col A, 1 ch, turn, dc (US sc) in first st and in each st across to last 2 loops of last st, bringing in col D in last 2 loops to complete last st, drop col A—25 dc (US sc).

Row 3: (skip unused dc [US sc] behind FPtr [US FPdc]) cont with col D, 1 ch, turn, dc (US sc) in first st, *work FPtr (US FPdc) around next st directly 2 rows below, dc (US sc) in next st, repeat from * across—12 x FPtr (US FPdc) in col D.

Row 4: cont with col D, repeat row 2, changing to col A—25 dc (US sc).

Row 5: (skip unused dc [US sc] behind FPdtr [US FPtr]) cont with col A, 1 ch, turn, dc (US sc) in first 2 sts, *work FPdtr (US FPtr) around next st directly 3 rows below, dc (US sc) in next st, repeat from * across, dc (US sc) in last 2 sts—11 x FPtr (US FPdc) in col A.

Row 6: cont with col A, repeat row 2, changing to col D—25 dc (US sc).

Row 7: (skip unused dc [US sc] behind FPdtr [US FPtr]) cont with col D, 1 ch, turn, dc (US sc) in first st, *work FPdtr (US FPtr) around next FPtr (US FPdc) directly 2 rows below, dc (US sc) in next st, repeat from * across—12 x FPdtr (US FPtr) in col D.

Row 8: cont with col D, repeat row 2, changing to col A—25 dc (US sc).

Row 9: (skip unused dc [US sc] behind FPdtr [US FPtr]) cont with col A, 1 ch,

Subsequent rows: repeat rows 2 to 13, alternating colours as required, ending with row 7, col B, finish off—4 x 5-spike groups.

Spike stitch: Insert hook into stitch indicated and draw up a long loop level with stitch on working row, YO and draw through 2 loops on hook—spike st made.

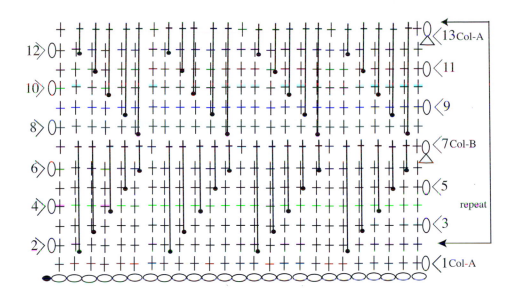

RELIEFS

Reliefs
Square 21

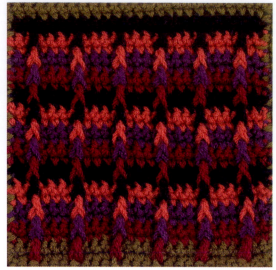

Colours A, B, C, D and E are required for this pattern.

With col A make 26 ch.

Row 1: cont col A, dc (US sc) in 2nd ch from hook and in each ch across—25 dc (US sc).

Row 2: (right side) cont with col A, 1 ch, turn, dc (US sc) in first and in each dc (US sc)—25 dc (US sc).

Row 3: cont col A, 1 ch, turn, dc (US sc) in first and in each st across to last 2 loops of last st, bringing in col B in last 2 loops to complete st, finish off col A—25 dc (US sc).

Row 4: skip unused dc (US sc) behind FPtr (US FPdc), cont with col B, 1 ch, turn, dc (US sc) in first 2 sts, *work FPtr (US FPdc) around next st directly 2 rows below, dc (US sc) in next 3 sts on working row, repeat from * across, dc (US sc) in each last 2 sts—6 x FPtr (US FPdc).

Row 5: cont with col B, repeat row 3, changing to col D—25 dc (US sc).

Row 6: skip unused dc (US sc) behind FPtr (US FPdc), cont with col D, 1 ch, turn, dc (US sc) in first 2 sts, *work FPtr (US FPdc) around next FPtr (US FPdc) directly 2 rows below, dc (US sc) in next 3 sts on working row, repeat from * across, dc (US sc) in last 2 sts—6 x FPtr (US FPdc).

Row 7: cont with col D, repeat row 3, changing to col C—25 dc (US sc).

Rows 8 and 9: cont with Col C, repeat

rows 6 and 7, changing to col E—25 dc
(US sc).

Rows 10 and 11: cont with Col E, repeat
rows 6 and 7, changing to col B—25 dc
(US sc).

Subsequent rows: repeat rows 6 and
7, repeating colour sequence B-D-C-E to
desired size, ending with row 3, col E,
bringing in col A in last 2 loops of last
st to complete st, then working 2 more
rows as follows.

Last 2 rows: cont with col A, 1 ch,
turn, dc (US sc) in first and in each st
across—25 dc (US sc).

**Front post treble (US front post
double crochet):** YO, insert hook from
front to back around post of stitch
indicated, (YO and draw through 2
loops) twice—FPtr (US FPdc) made.

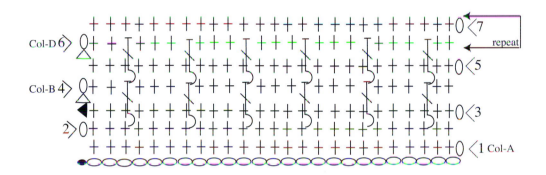

Colours A and D are required for this pattern.

With col A make 27 ch.

Row 1: (right side) cont with col A, tr in 4th ch from hook and in each ch across—25 tr.

Row 2: cont with col A, 1 ch, turn, dc (US sc) in first st and in each st across to last 2 loops of last st, bringing in col D in last 2 loops to complete last st, drop col A—25 dc (US sc).

Row 3: (skip unused dc [US sc] behind FPtr [US FPdc]) cont with col D, 1 ch, turn, dc (US sc) in first st, *work FPtr (US FPdc) around next st directly 2 rows below, dc (US sc) in next st, repeat from * across—12 x FPtr (US FPdc) in col D.

Row 4: cont with col D, repeat row 2, changing to col A—25 dc (US sc).

Row 5: (skip unused dc [US sc] behind FPdtr [US FPtr]) cont with col A, 1 ch, turn, dc (US sc) in first 2 sts, *work FPdtr (US FPtr) around next st directly 3 rows below, dc (US sc) in next st, repeat from * across, dc (US sc) in last 2 sts—11 x FPtr (US FPdc) in col A.

Row 6: cont with col A, repeat row 2, changing to col D—25 dc (US sc).

Row 7: (skip unused dc [US sc] behind FPdtr [US FPtr]) cont with col D, 1 ch, turn, dc (US sc) in first st, *work FPdtr (US FPtr) around next FPtr (US FPdc) directly 2 rows below, dc (US sc) in next st, repeat from * across—12 x FPdtr (US FPtr) in col D.

Row 8: cont with col D, repeat row 2, changing to col A—25 dc (US sc).

Row 9: (skip unused dc [US sc] behind FPdtr [US FPtr]) cont with col A, 1 ch, turn, dc (US sc) in first 2 sts, *work FPdtr (US FPtr) around next FPdtr (US FPtr) directly 2 rows below, dc (US sc) in next st, repeat from * across, dc (US sc) in last 2 sts—11 x FPdtr (US FPtr) in col A.

Row 10: cont with col A, repeat row 2, changing to col D—25 dc (US sc).

Row 11: (skip unused dc [US sc] behind FPdtr [US FPtr]) cont with col D, 1 ch, turn, dc (US sc) in first st, *work FPdtr (US FPtr) around next FPdtr (US FPtr) directly 2 rows below, dc (US sc) in next st, repeat from * across—12 x FPdtr (US FPtr) in col D.

Row 12: cont with col D, repeat row 2, changing to col A—25 dc (US sc).

Subsequent rows: repeat rows 9 to 12, ending with row 10, col A, and a last row as follows.

Last row: cont with col A, 1 ch, turn, dc (US sc) in first and in each st across, finish off.

Front post treble (US front post double crochet): YO, insert hook from front to back around post of stitch indicated, (YO and draw through 2 loops) twice—FPtr (US FPdc) made.

Front post double treble (US front post treble): (YO) twice, insert hook from front to back around post of stitch indicated, YO and draw up a loop, (YO and draw through 2 loops) 3 times— FPdtr (US FPtr) made.

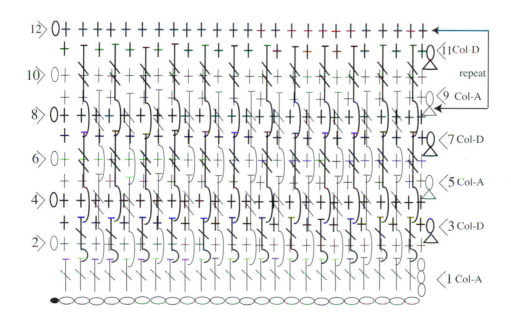

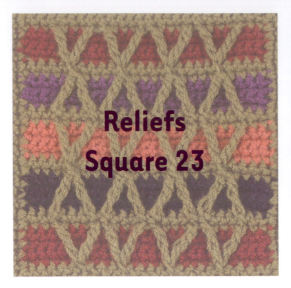

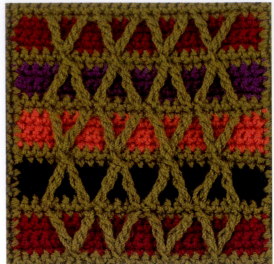

Reliefs Square 23

Colours A, B, C, D and E are required for this pattern.

With col A make 26 ch.

Row 1: (wrong side) cont with col A, dc (US sc) in 2nd ch from hook and in each ch across to last 2 loops of last st, bringing in col B in last 2 loops of last st to complete st, drop col A—25 dc (US sc).

Rows 2 to 4: cont with col B, 1 ch, turn, dc (US sc) in first and in each st across—25 dc (US sc).

Row 5: cont with col B, 1 ch, turn, dc (US sc) in first and in each st across to last 2 loops of last st, bringing in col A in last 2 loops to complete st, finish off Col B—25 dc (US sc).

Row 6: (skip unused dc [US sc] behind FPdtr [US FPtr]) cont with col A, 1 ch,

turn, dc (US sc) in first 2 sts, work FPdtr (US FPtr) around dc (US sc) 3 sts forward 5 rows below, dc (US sc) in next 3 sts on working row, *work FPdtr (US FPtr) in same st as last FPdtr (US FPtr) 5 rows below, work FPdtr (US FPtr) around dc (US sc) 5 sts forward from last FPdtr (US FPtr) 5 rows below, dc (US sc) in next 3 sts on working row, repeat from * across—8 x FPdtr (US FPtr).

Row 7: cont with col A, repeat row 2, changing to col E, drop col A—25 dc (US sc).

Rows 8 to 11: cont with col E, repeat rows 2 to 5, changing to col A, finish off col E—25 dc (US sc).

Row 12: (skip unused dc [US sc] behind FPdtr [US FPtr] relief cluster) cont with col A, 1 ch, turn, dc (US sc) in first 4 sts, *work FPdtr (US FPtr) relief cluster around dc (US sc) directly above each next 2 FPdtr (US FPtr) 5 rows below, dc (US sc) in next 4 sts on working row, repeat from * across, dc (US sc) in last st—4 x FPdtr (US FPtr) relief clusters.

Row 13: cont with col A, repeat row 2, changing to col C, drop col A—25 dc (US sc).

Rows 14 to 17: cont with Col C, repeat rows 2 to 5, changing to col A, finish off col C—25 dc (US sc).

Row 18: (skip unused dc [US sc] behind FPdtr [US FPtr]) cont with col A, 1 ch, turn, dc (US sc) in first 2 sts, work FPdtr (US FPtr) around top of first relief

cluster 6 rows below, dc (US sc) in next 3 sts on working row, *work FPdtr (US FPtr) in same st as last FPdtr (US FPtr), work FPdtr (US FPtr) around top of next relief cluster 6 rows below, dc (US sc) in next 3 sts on working row, repeat from * across to last 3 sts, dc (US sc) in each last 3 sts—8 x FPdtr (US FPtr).

Row 19: cont with col A, repeat row 2, changing to col D, drop col A—25 dc (US sc).

Subsequent Rows: repeat rows 8 to 19 alternating colours in following colour sequence: AB AE AC AD ABA ending with Row 19 Col-A, finish off—25 dc.

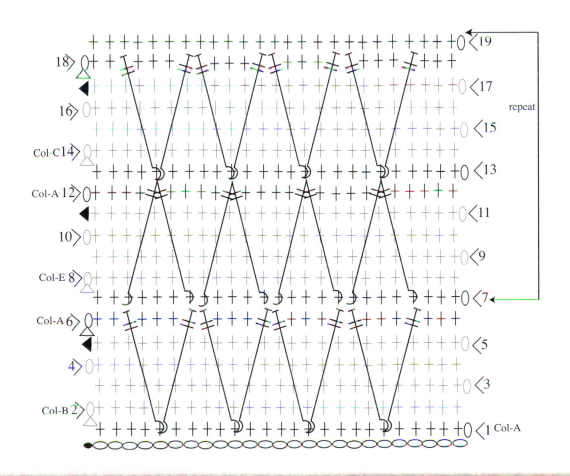

Front post treble (US front post double crochet): YO, insert hook from front to back around post of stitch indicated, (YO and draw through 2 loops) twice—FPtr (US FPdc) made.

Front post double treble relief cluster stitch (US front post treble) relief cluster: *YO twice, insert hook around post of stitch indicated and draw up a loop, (YO and draw through 2 loops on hook) twice, repeat from * once more in next stitch indicated (3 loops on hook), YO and draw through 3 loops—FPdtr (US FPtr) relief cluster made.

Front post double treble (US front post treble): YO twice, insert hook from front to back around post of stitch indicated, (YO and draw through 2 loops) 3 times—FPdtr (US FPtr) made.

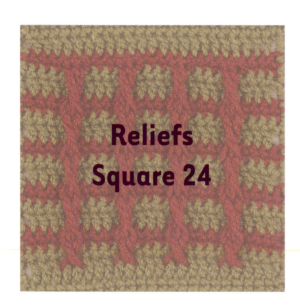

Colours A and B are required for this pattern.

With col A make 27 ch.

Row 1: (right side) cont with col A, tr (US dc) in 4th ch from hook and in each ch across—25 tr (US dc).

Row 2: cont with col A, 1 ch, turn, dc (US sc) in first and in each st across to last 2 loops of last st, bringing in col B in last 2 loops to complete st, drop col A—25 dc (US sc).

Row 3: (skip unused dc [US sc] behind twisted cable st) cont with col B, 1 ch, turn, dc (US sc) in first 4 sts, *work twisted cable st directly 2 rows below, dc (US sc) in next 3 st, repeat from * across to last st, dc (US sc) in last st—4 x twisted cables.

Row 4: cont with col B, repeat row 2, changing to col A—25 dc (US sc).

Row 5: cont with col A, 3 ch (count as tr [US dc]), turn, tr (US dc) in next and in each st across—25 tr (US dc).

Row 6: cont with col, A repeat row 2, changing to col B—25 dc (US sc).

Row 7: (skip unused dc [US sc] behind twisted cable st) cont with col B, 1 ch, turn, dc (US sc) in first 4 sts, *work twisted cable st directly 4 rows below, dc (US sc) in next 3 sts, repeat from * across to last st, dc (US sc) in last st—4 x twisted cables.

Row 8: cont with col B, repeat row 2, changing to col A—25 dc (US sc).

Subsequent rows: repeat rows 5 to 8, ending with row 5, col A, finish off—25 tr (US dc).

Front post double treble (US front post treble): (YO) twice, insert hook from front to back around post of stitch indicated, YO and draw up a loop, (YO and draw through 2 loops) 3 times—FPdtr (US FPtr) made.

Twisted cable stitch: (worked over 2 sts) skip next st, work FPdtr (US FPtr) around next st directly below on row indicated, work FPdtr (US FPtr) around skipped st on same row—twisted cable made.

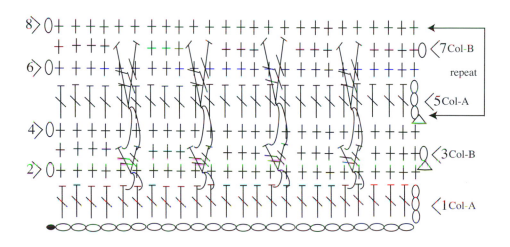

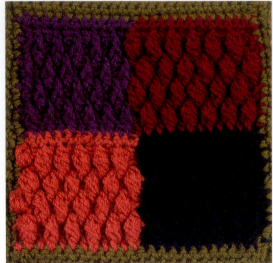

Colours A, B, C, D and E are required for this pattern.

1ST HALF

With col A make 26 ch.

Row 1: cont col A, dc (US sc) in 2nd ch from hook and in each ch across to last 2 loops of last st, bringing in col E in last 2 loops to complete st, finish off col A—25 dc (US sc).

Row 2: (right side) cont with col E, 3 ch (count as tr [US dc]), turn, tr (US dc) in next 12 sts, bringing in col C in last 2 loops of last tr (US dc) to complete st, drop col E, cont with col C, tr (US dc) in next 12 sts—13 tr (US dc) col E + 12 tr (US dc) col C.

Row 3: cont with col C, 1 ch, turn, dc (US sc) in first and next 11 sts, bringing in col E in last 2 loops of last dc (US sc) to complete st, drop col C, cont with col

E, dc (US sc) in next 13 sts—13 dc (US sc) col E + 12 dc (US sc) col C.

Row 4: (skip unused sts behind FPtr [US FPdc] and FP cluster) cont with col E, 3 ch, turn, *work FPtr (US FPdc) around next st directly 2 rows below, tr (US dc) in next st on working row, repeat from * 5 times more, bringing in col C in last 2 loops of last tr (US dc) to complete st, drop col E, cont with col C, **work FP cluster around next st directly 2 rows below, tr (US dc) in next st on working row, repeat from ** 5 times more—6 x FPtr (US FPdc) col E + 6 x FP clusters col C.

Row 5: repeat row 3—13 dc (US sc) col E + 12 dc (US sc) col C.

Row6: (skip unused sts behind FPtr [US FPdc] and FP cluster) cont with col E, 3 ch, turn, *tr (US dc) in next st on working row, work FPtr (US FPdc)

around next st directly 2 rows below, repeat from * 5 times more, bringing in col C in last 2 loops of last tr (US dc) to complete st, drop col E, cont with col C, **tr (US dc) in next st on working row, work FP cluster around next st directly 2 rows below, repeat from ** 5 times more—6 x FPtr (US FPdc) col E + 6 x FP clusters col C.

Row 7: repeat row 3—13 dc (US sc) col E + 12 dc (US sc) col C.

Rows 8 to 11: repeat rows 4 to 7 to last 2 loops of last st, bringing in col B in last 2 loops to complete st, finish off both col E and col C.

2ND HALF

Row 12: cont with col B, 3 ch, turn, tr (US dc) in next 12 sts, bringing in col D in last 2 loops of last tr (US dc) to complete st, drop col B, cont with col D, tr (US dc) in next 12 sts—13 tr (US dc) col B + 12 tr (US dc) col D.

Row 13: cont with col D, 1 ch, turn, dc (US sc) in first and next 11 sts, bringing in col B in last 2 loops of last dc (US sc) to complete st, drop col D, cont with col B, dc (US sc) in next 13 sts—13 dc (US sc) col B + 12 dc (US sc) col D.

Row 14: (skip unused sts behind FPtr [US FPdc] and FP cluster) cont with col B, 3 ch, turn, *work FP cluster around

next st directly 2 rows below, tr (US dc) in next st on working row, repeat from * 5 times more, bringing in col D in last 2 loops of last tr (US dc) to complete st, drop col B, cont with col D, **work FPtr (US FPdc) around next st directly 2 rows below, tr (US dc) in next st on working row, repeat from ** 5 times more—6 x FP clusters col B + 6 x FPtr (US FPdc) col D.

Row 15: repeat row 13—13 dc (US sc) col B + 12 dc (US sc) col D.

Row 16: (skip unused sts behind FPtr [US FPdc] and FP cluster) cont with col B, 3 ch, turn, *tr (US dc) in next st on working row, work FP cluster around next st directly 2 rows below, repeat from * 5 times more, bringing in col D in last 4 loops of last FP cluster to complete st, drop col B, cont with col D, **tr (US dc) in next st on working row, work FPtr (US FPdc) around next st directly 2 rows below, repeat from ** 5 times more, tr (US dc) in last st—6 x FP clusters col B + 6 x FPtr (US FPdc) col D.

Row 17: repeat row 13—13 dc (US sc) col B + 12 dc (US sc) col D.

Rows 18 to 21: repeat rows 14 to 17 to last 2 loops of last st, bringing in col A in last 2 loops to complete st, finish off both col B and col D, then work 2 more rows as follows.

Last 2 rows: cont with col A, 1 ch, dc (US sc) in first and in each st across, finish off.

Front post treble (US front post double crochet): YO, insert hook from front to back around post of stitch indicated and draw up a loop, (YO and draw through 2 loops) twice—FPtr (US FPdc) made.

Front post cluster: (YO, insert hook from front to back around post of st indicated and draw up a loop, YO and draw through 2 loops) 3 times, YO and draw through all 4 loops on hook—FP cluster made.

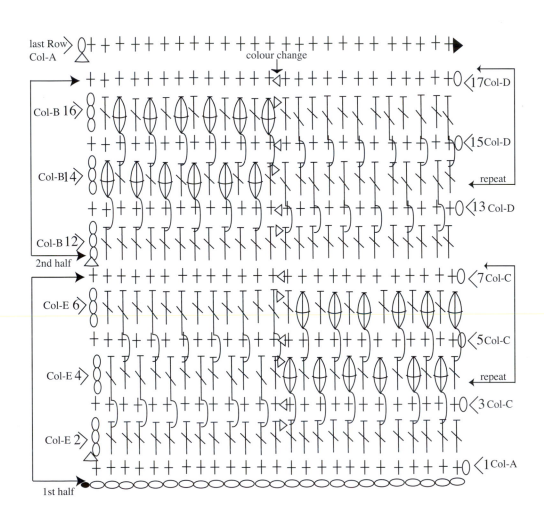

RIPPLES

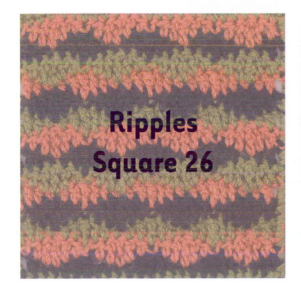

Ripples
Square 26

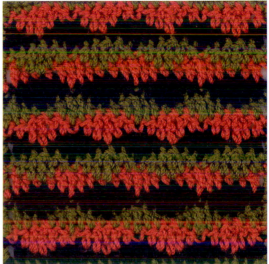

Colours A, C and E are required for this pattern.

With col A make 26 ch.

Row 1: cont with col A, dc (US sc) in 2nd ch from hook and in each ch across to last 2 loops of last st, bringing in col E in last 2 loops to complete last st, drop col A—25 dc (US sc).

Row 2: (right side) cont with col E, 4 ch (count as dtr [US tr]), turn, tr (US dc) in next st, htr (US hdc) in next st, dc (US sc) in next st, *htr (US hdc) in next st, tr (US dc) in next st, dtr (US tr) in next st, tr (US dc) in next st, htr (US hdc) in next st, dc (US sc) in next st, repeat from * across to last 3 sts, htr (US hdc) in next st, tr (US dc) in next st, dtr (US tr) in last st, bringing in col C in last 2 loops of st to complete st, drop col E—25 sts.

Row 3: cont with col C, 1 ch, turn, dc (US sc) in first st, *htr (US hdc) in next st, tr (US dc) in next st, dtr (US tr) in next st, tr (US dc) in next st, htr (US hdc) in next st, dc (US sc) in next st, repeat from * across to last 4 sts, dtr (US tr) in next st, tr (US dc) in next st, dc (US sc) in last st, bringing in col A in last 2 loops of st to complete st, drop col C—25 sts.

Row 4: cont with col A, repeat row 2, changing to col E—25 sts.

Row 5: cont with col E, repeat row 3, changing to col C—25 sts.

Subsequent rows: repeat rows 2 and 3, alternating colours as required, ending with row 3, col C, then 2 more rows as follows.

Last 2 rows: cont with col A, 1 ch, turn, dc (US sc) in first st and in each st across—25 dc (US sc).

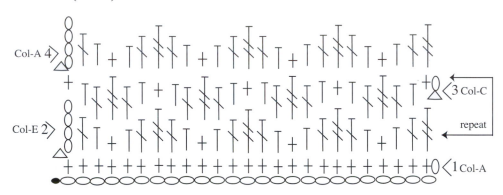

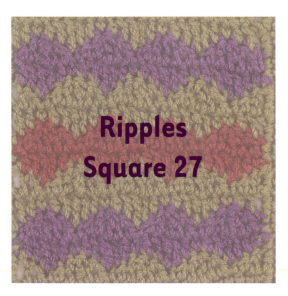

Ripples
Square 27

Colours A, B and D are required for this pattern.

With col A make 26 ch.

Row 1: (right side) cont with col A, dc (US sc) in 2nd ch from hook and in each ch across—25 dc (US sc).

Row 2: cont with col A, 4 ch (count as dtr [US tr]), turn, tr (US dc) in next st, htr (US hdc) in next st, dc (US sc) in next st, *htr (US hdc) in next st, tr (US dc) in next st, dtr (US tr) in next st, tr (US dc) in next st, htr (US hdc) in next st, dc (US sc) in next st, repeat from * across to last 3 sts, htr (US hdc) in next st, tr (US dc) in next st, dtr (US tr) in next st, bringing in col D in last 2 loops of st to complete st, drop col A—25 sts.

Row 3: cont with col D, 1 ch, turn, dc (US sc) in first st, *htr (US hdc) in next st, tr (US dc) in next st, dtr (US tr) in next st, tr (US dc) in next st, htr (US hdc) in next st, dc (US sc) in next st, repeat from * across—25 sts.

Row 4: cont with col D, repeat row 3, changing to col A, finish off col D—25 sts.

Row 5: cont with col A, repeat row 2—25 sts.

Row 6: cont with col A, repeat row 2, changing to col B, finish off col A—25 sts.

Row 7: cont with col B, repeat row 3—25 sts.

Row 8: cont with col B, repeat row 3, changing to col A, finish off col B—25 sts.

Subsequent rows: repeat rows 3 to 6, alternating colours as required, ending with row 5, col A, do not finish off—25 sts.

Last row: cont with col A, 1 ch, turn, dc (US sc) in first and in each st across, finish off—25 dc (US sc).

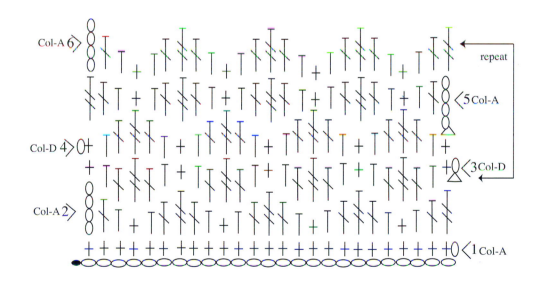

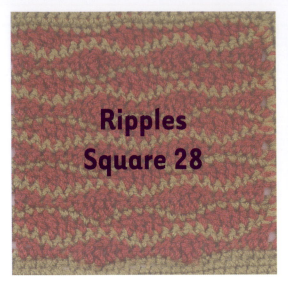

Ripples
Square 28

Colours A and B are required for this pattern.

With col A make 26 ch.

Row 1: (right side) cont with col A, dc (US sc) in 2nd ch from hook and in each ch across to last 2 loops of last st, bringing in col B in last 2 loops to complete last st, drop col A—25 dc (US sc).

Row 2: cont with col B, 4 ch (count as dtr [US tr], beginning ch), turn, tr (US dc) in next st, htr (US hdc) in next st, dc (US sc) in next 3 sts, *htr (US hdc) in next st, tr (US dc) in next st, dtr (US tr) in next st, tr (US dc) in next st, htr (US hdc) in next st, dc (US sc) in next 3 sts, repeat from * across to last 3 sts, htr (US hdc) in next st, tr (US dc) in next st, dtr (US tr) in last st, drop col B—25 sts.

Row 3: do not turn, remove hook and reinsert into 4th ch of beginning ch of same row and bring in col A, 1 ch, dc (US sc) in same st and in each st across to last 2 loops of last dc (US sc), bringing in col B in last 2 loops to complete last st, drop col A—25 dc (US sc).

Row 4: cont with col B, 1 ch, turn, dc (US sc) in first 2 sts, *htr (US hdc) in next st, tr (US dc) in next st, dtr (US tr) in next st, tr (US dc) in next st, htr (US hdc) in next st, dc (US sc) in next 3 sts, repeat from * across to last 2 sts, dc (US sc) in last 2 sts, drop col B—25 sts.

Row 5: do not turn, remove hook and reinsert into first dc (US sc) of same row and bring in col A, 1 ch, dc (US sc) in same st and in each st across to last 2 loops of last st, bringing in col B in last 2 loops to complete last st, drop col A—25 dc (US sc).

Subsequent rows: repeat rows 2 to 5, ending with row 5, col A, do not finish off.

Last row: cont with col A, 1 ch, turn, dc (US sc) in first and in each st across, finish off—25 dc (US sc).

Colours A, B, C, D and E are required for this pattern.

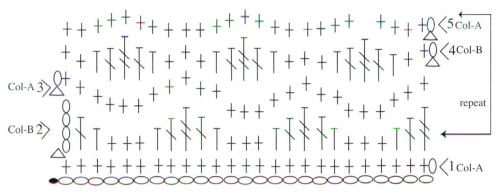

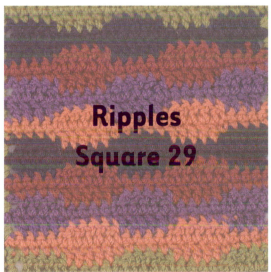

Ripples
Square 29

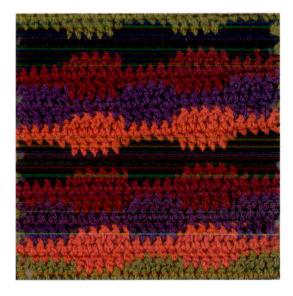

With col A make 26 ch.

Row 1: (right side) cont with col A, dc (US sc) in 2nd ch from hook and in each ch across—25 dc (US sc).

Row 2: cont with col A, 3 ch (count as tr [US dc]), turn, tr (US dc) in next 4 sts, *dc (US sc) in next 5 sts, tr (US dc) in next 5 sts, repeat from * across to last

2 loops of last st, bringing in col C in last 2 loops to complete st, finish off col A—25 sts.

Row 3: cont with col C, 1 ch, turn, dc (US sc) in first 5 sts, *tr (US dc) in next 5 sts, dc (US sc) in next 5 sts, repeat from * across—25 sts.

Row 4: cont with col C, repeat row 3,

changing to col D, finish off col C—25 sts.

Row 5: cont with col D, repeat row 2—25 sts.

Row 6: cont with col D, repeat row 2, changing to col B, finish off col D—25 sts.

Subsequent rows: repeat rows 3 to 6, alternating colours as required in the sequence A-C-D-B-E-A, ending with row 3, col A, do not finish off.

Last row: cont with col A, 1 ch, turn, dc (US sc) in first and in each st across, finish off—25 dc (US sc).

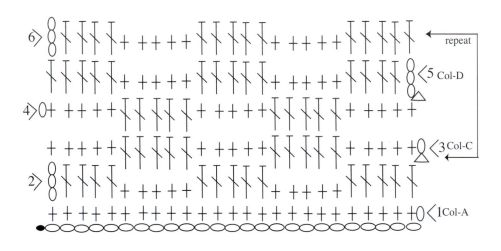

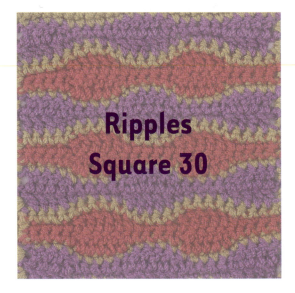

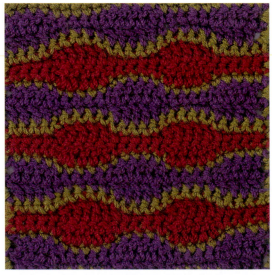

Ripples
Square 30

Colours A, B and D are required for this pattern.

With col A make 26 ch.

Row 1: (right side) cont with col A, dc (US sc) in 2nd ch from hook and in each ch across to last 2 loops of last dc (US sc), bringing in col D in last 2 loops of last st to complete st, drop col A—25 dc (US sc).

Row 2: cont with col D, 3 ch (count as tr [US dc]), turn, tr (US dc) in next 4 sts, *dc (US sc) in next 5 sts, tr (US dc) in next 5 sts, repeat from * across—25 sts.

Row 3: cont with col D, repeat row 2, bringing in col A in last 2 loops of last st to complete st, finish off col D—25 sts.

Row 4: cont with col A, 1 ch, turn, dc (US sc) in first st and in each st across to last 2 loops of last st, bringing in col B in last 2 loops to complete st, drop col A—25 dc (US sc).

Row 5: cont with Col B, 1 ch, turn, dc (US sc) in first 5 sts, *tr (US dc) in next 5 sts, dc (US sc) in next 5 sts, repeat from * across—25 sts.

Row 6: cont with col B, repeat row 5, bringing in col A in last 2 loops of last st to complete st, finish off col B—25 sts.

Row 7: cont with col A, repeat row 4, bringing in col D in last 2 loops of last st to complete st, drop col A—25 dc (US sc).

Subsequent rows: repeat rows 2 to 7, alternating colours in the sequence A-D-B, ending with row 7, col A.

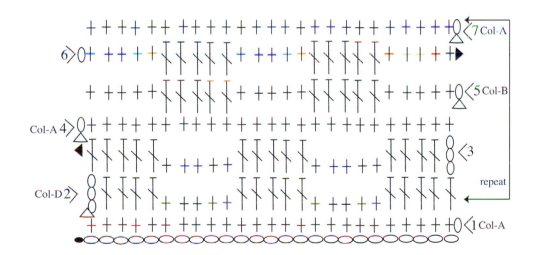

CHAINS

Chains Square 31

Colours A, B, C, D and E are required for this pattern.

With col A make 26 ch.

Row 1: (right side) cont with col A, dc (US sc) in 2nd ch from hook and in each ch across—25 dc (US sc).

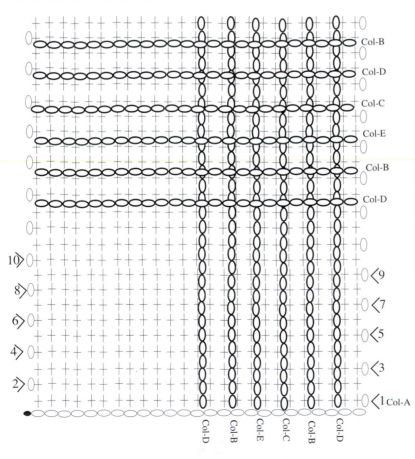

Refer to diagram for placement of colours B, C, D and E and work surface slip st over square just made.

Row 2: cont with col A, 1 ch, turn, dc (US sc) in first st and in each st across—25 dc (US sc).

Subsequent rows: repeat row 2 with col A until a square is made (approx 25 rows), finish off—25 dc (US sc).

Surface slip stitch: beginning at bottom, with right side facing and yarn at back, insert hook into sp between two sts and draw up a loop, *insert hook in next sp between 2 sts above st just made and draw up a loop through base-fabric and loop on hook, repeat from * to end, finish off and weave in tail-ends on wrong side.

Colours A and D are required for this pattern.

With col A make 26 ch.

Row 1: (right side) cont with col A, htr (US hdc) in 3rd ch from hook and in each ch across, drop col A—25 htr (US hdc).

Row 2: do not turn, remove hook and reinsert in top of 2-ch beginning ch of same row and bring in col D, 1 ch, dc

(US sc) in first 8 sts, 13 ch, skip next 9 sts, dc (US sc) in last 8 sts, bringing in col A in last 2 loops of last st to complete st, drop col D—16 x dc (US sc) + 9 skipped sts + 1 x 13-ch loops.

Row 3: cont with col A, 2 ch (count as htr [US hdc], beginning ch), turn, htr (US hdc) in next 7 sts, [working in front of 13-ch loop] tr (US dc) in next 9 skipped sts, htr (US hdc) in last 8 sts, drop col A—16 x htr (US hdc) + 9 x tr (US dc).

Row 4: do not turn, remove hook and reinsert in top of 2-ch beginning ch of same row and bring in col D, 1 ch, dc (US sc) in first 8 sts, 13 ch, skip next 9 sts, dc (US sc) in last 8 sts, bringing in col A in last 2 loops of last st to complete st, drop col D—16 x dc (US sc) + 9 skipped sts + 1 x 13-ch loops.

Row 5: cont with col A, repeat row 3 (working behind 13-ch loop)—16 x htr (US hdc) + 9 x tr (US dc).

Rows 6 to 9: repeat rows 2 to 5 once more.

Row 10: do not turn, remove hook and reinsert in top of 2-ch beginning ch of same row and bring in col D, 1 ch, dc (US sc) in first 8 sts, 6 ch, (working over and around all 4 x 13-ch loops) insert

hook from front to back, gather up loops and make 1 dc (US sc), 6 ch, skip next 9 sts, dc (US sc) in last 8 sts, bringing in col A in last 2 loops of last st to complete st, finish off col D—17 x dc (US sc) + 9 skipped sts + 2 x 6-ch loops.

Row 11: cont with col A, repeat row 3 (working in front of 13-ch loop)—16 x htr (US hdc) + 9 x tr (US dc).

Row 12: 2 ch, htr (US hdc) in next st and each st across—25 htr (US hdc).

Subsequent rows: repeat rows 2 to 12 once more, finish off.

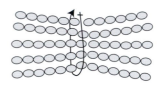

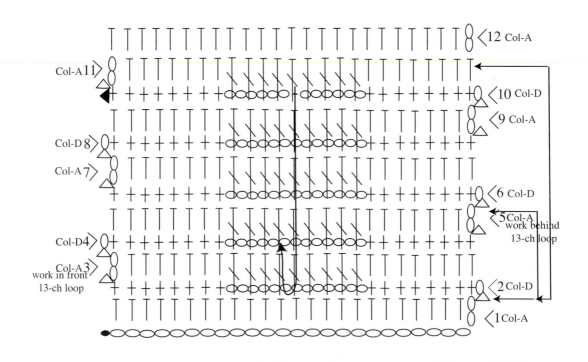

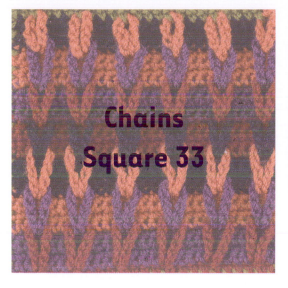

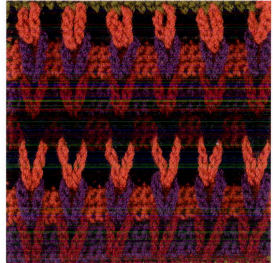

Colours A, B, C, D and E are required for this pattern.

With col A make 26 ch.

Row 1: cont with col A, dc (US sc) in 2nd ch from hook and in each ch across to last 2 loops of last st, bringing in col B in last 2 loops to complete st, finish off col A—25 dc (US sc).

Row 2: (right side) cont with col B, 1 ch, turn, dc (US sc) in first 2 sts, *12 ch, dc (US sc) in next 4 sts, repeat from * across to last 3 sts, dc (US sc) in last 3 sts, bringing in col D in last 2 loops of last st to complete st, finish off col B—6 x 12-ch loops in col B.

From now on, keep 12-ch loops on right side by working in front or back of 12-ch loops as required.

Rows 3 to 5: cont with col D, 1 ch, turn, dc (US sc) in first and in each st across—25 dc (US sc).

Row 6: cont with col D, repeat row 2 to last 2 loops of last st, bringing in col C in last 2 loops to complete st, finish off col D—6 x 12-ch loops in col D.

Subsequent rows: repeat rows 3 to 6, alternating colours in the sequence A-B-D-C-E, ending with rows 3 to 5 in col E to last 2 loops of last st, bringing in col A in last 2 loops to complete st, finish off col E, then work a last row as follows.

Before working last row: with right side facing and starting from the bottom-up, manually thread 12-ch loops together by bringing each loop through the one below, repeat for each 6 columns of 12-ch loops.

Last row: cont with col A, 1 ch, turn, dc (US sc) in first 2 sts, *insert hook under 12-ch loop and dc (US sc) in next dc (US sc) around 12-ch loop, dc (US sc) in next 3 sts, repeat from * across to last 2 sts, dc (US sc) in last 2 sts, finish off—25 dc (US sc).

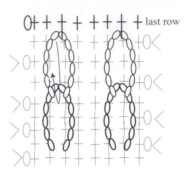

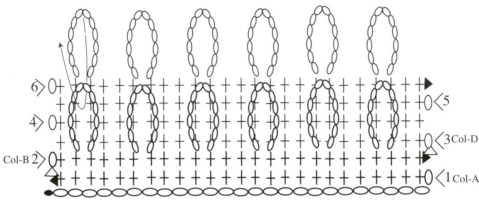

Chains Square 34

Colours A and E are required for this pattern.

With col A make 26 ch.

Row 1: (right side) cont with col A, dc (US sc) in 2nd ch from hook and in each ch across—25 dc (US sc).

Row 2: cont with col A, 1 ch, turn, dc (US sc) in first st, *cluster st in next st, dc (US sc) in next 3 sts, repeat from * across—6 x clusters.

Row 3: cont with col A, 1 ch, turn, dc (US sc) in first and in each st across—25 dc (US sc).

Row 4: cont col A, 1 ch, turn, dc (US sc) in first 2 sts, *cluster st in next st, dc (US sc) in next 3 sts, repeat from * across, dc (US sc) in last 2 sts—6 x clusters.

Row 5: cont col A, repeat row 3—25 dc (US sc).

Row 6: cont col A, 1 ch, turn, dc (US sc) in first 3 sts, *cluster st in next st, dc (US sc) in next 3 sts, repeat from * across, dc (US sc) in last st—6 x clusters.

Row 7: cont col A, repeat row 3—25 dc (US sc).

Subsequent rows: cont with col A, repeat rows 2 to 7 until a square is made, ending with row 3, finish off—25 dc (US sc).

Complete square with surface slip stitch as shown in diagram and photograph.

Surface slip stitch: with col E, begin at bottom, with right side facing and yarn at back, insert hook into sp between two sts and draw up a loop, *working diagonally between cluster sts, insert hook in next sp between 2 sts above st just made and draw up a loop through base-fabric and loop on hook, repeat from * to end, finish off and weave in tail-ends on wrong side.

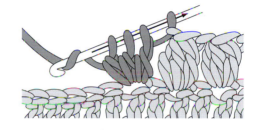

Cluster stitch: YO, insert hook in stitch or space and pull up a loop, YO and draw through 2 loops on hook) 3 times, YO and draw through all 4 loops on hook—cluster made.

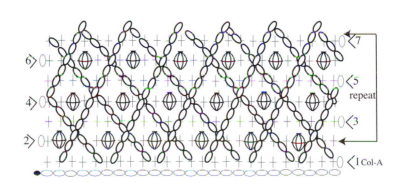

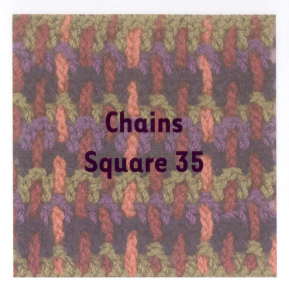

Chains
Square 35

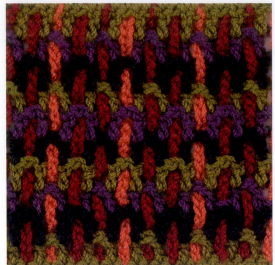

Colours A, B, C, D and E are required for this pattern.

With col A make 26 ch.

Row 1: (right side) cont with col A, dc (US sc) in 2nd ch from hook and in each ch across—25 dc (US sc).

Row 2: cont with col A, 4 ch [count as tr (US dc) + 1ch], turn, tr (US dc) in next st, *1 ch, skip next st, tr (US dc) in next st, repeat from * across to last 2 loops of last st, bringing in col E in last 2 loops to complete last st, drop col A—13 tr (US dc) + 12 x 1-ch sps.

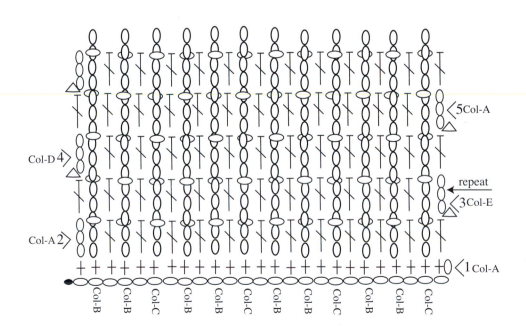

Row 3: cont with col E, 4 ch, turn, tr (US dc) in next st, *1 ch, skip 1-ch sp, tr (US dc) in next st, repeat from * across to beginning 4-ch, tr (US dc) in 3rd ch of beginning ch, bringing in col D in last 2 loops of last st to complete st, drop col E—13 tr (US dc) + 12 x 1-ch sps.

Row 4: cont with col D, repeat row 3, changing to col A.

Subsequent rows: repeat row 3, alternating colours in the sequence A-E-D, ending with col A.

Complete square with surface decoration as shown in diagram and photograph.

- Make 8 x lengths of chain in col B to fit square.
- Make 4 x lengths of chain in col C to fit square.
- Starting from the bottom up, thread chain lengths, under and over, through each 1-ch sp in colour sequence B-B-C—12 x threaded 1-ch sps.
- Weave in tail-ends on wrong side.

MOSAICS

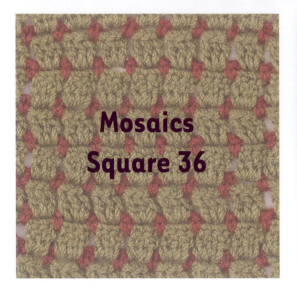

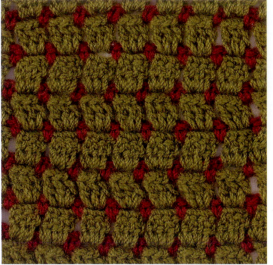

Colours A and B are required for this pattern.

With col A make 27 ch.

Row 1: (right side) cont with col A, tr (US dc) in 4th ch from hook, 1 ch, *tr (US dc) in next 3 ch, 1 ch, repeat from * across to last 2 ch, tr (US dc) in next ch, tr (US dc) in last ch, bringing in col B in last 2 loops of last st to complete st, drop col A—25 tr (US dc) + 8 x 1-ch sps.

Row 2: cont with col B, 2 ch (count as beginning ch), turn, *dc (US sc) in 1-ch sp, 2 ch, repeat from * across to last 2 sts, skip next st, ss into top of beginning ch, drop col B—8 dc (US sc) + 9 x 2-ch sps.

Row 3: do not turn, remove hook and reinsert hook into first st of 2-ch beginning ch of same row and bring in Col A, 3 ch (count as tr [US dc]), tr (US dc) in first 2-ch sp, 1 ch, *3 tr (US dc) in next 2-ch sp, 1 ch, repeat across to last 2-ch sp, 2 tr (US dc) in last 2-ch sp, bringing in col B in last 2 loops of last st to complete st, drop col A—25 tr (US dc) + 8 x 1-ch sps.

Subsequent rows: repeat rows 2 and 3, ending with row 3, col A, as follows.

Last row: do not turn, remove hook and reinsert hook into top of beginning ch of same row and bring in col A, 3 ch, tr (US dc) in first 2-ch sp, *3 tr (US dc) in next 2-ch sp, repeat across to last 2-ch sp, 2 tr (US dc) in last 2-ch sp finish off—25 tr (US dc).

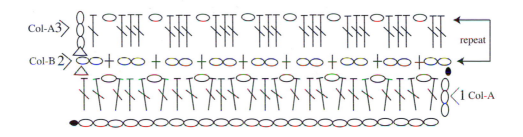

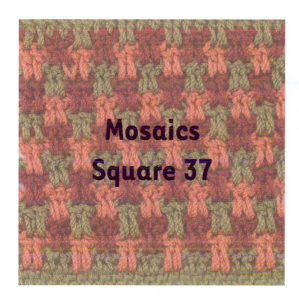

Mosaics
Square 37

Colours A, B and C are required for this pattern.

With col A make 26 ch.

Row 1: (right side) cont with col A, dc (US sc) into 2nd ch from hook and in each ch—25 dc (US sc).

Row 2: cont with col A, 5 ch (count as tr [US dc] + 2 ch), turn, skip next 2 sts, *tr (US dc) in next 2 sts, 2 ch, skip next 2 sts, repeat from * across to last 2 loops of last st, bringing in col C in last

2 loops to complete st, drop col A—6 x 2-ch sps.

Row 3: cont with col C, 4 ch [count as tr (US dc) + 1 ch], turn, skip next st, *working over next 2-ch sp work Ltr (US Ldc) in next 2 skipped sts 2 rows below, 2 ch, skip next 2 sts, repeat from * across, tr (US dc) in last st (3rd ch of 5-ch beginning ch), bringing in col B in last 2 loops of last st to complete st, drop col C—5 x 2-ch sps + 1 x 1-ch sp.

Row 4: cont with col B, 5 ch, turn, skip

next 2 sts, *working over next 2-ch sp work Ltr (US Ldc) in next 2 skipped sts 2 rows below, 2 ch, skip next 2 sts, repeat from * across to last 1-ch sp, working over last 1-ch sp, work Ltr (US Ldc) in next skipped st 2 rows below, tr (US dc) in 3rd ch of 4-ch beginning ch, bringing in col A in last 2 loops of last st to complete st, drop col B—6 x 2-ch sps.

Subsequent rows: repeat rows 3 and 4, alternating colours in the sequence A-C-B-A, ending with a last row in col A as follows.

Last row: cont with col A, 1 ch, turn, dc (US sc) in each st and Ltr (US Ldc) in each skipped st 2 rows below across, finish off—25 sts.

Long treble (US long double crochet): YO, insert hook into st indicated and draw up a long loop level with st on working row, (YO and draw through 2 loops) twice—Ltr (US Ldc) made.

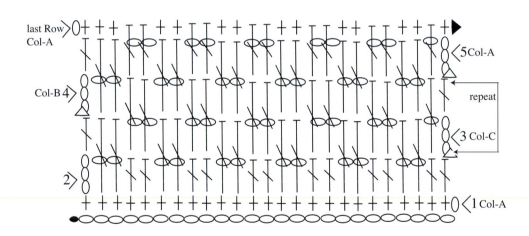

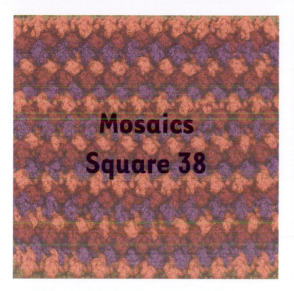

Mosaics
Square 38

Colours A, B, C and D are required for this pattern.

With col A make 26 ch.

Row 1: (right side) cont with col A, dc (US sc) into 2nd ch from hook and in each ch across to last 2 loops of last st, bringing in col C in last 2 loops to complete st, finish off col A—25 dc (US sc).

Row 2: cont with col C, 1 ch, turn, dc (US sc) in first st, *dtr (US tr) in next st, dc (US sc) in next st, repeat from * across to last 2 loops of last st, bringing in col D in last 2 loops to complete st, drop col C—25 sts.

Row 3: cont with col D, 1 ch, turn, dc (US sc) in first 2 sts, *dtr (US tr) in next st, dc (US sc) in next st, repeat from * across to last 2 sts, dc (US sc) in last 2 sts, bringing in col B in last 2 loops of last st to complete st—25 sts.

- This is a wide pattern, work tightly or use a smaller hook to stay in line with other 63 squares.
- Keep dtr (US tr) to front of work.

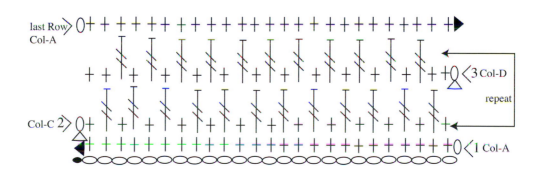

Subsequent rows: repeat rows 2 and 3, alternating colours in the sequence C-D-B, ending with a col C row (2 or 3), and bringing in col A in last 2 loops of last st to complete st, then working a last row as follows.

Last row: cont with col A, 1 ch, turn, dc (US sc) in first and in each st across, finish off—25 dc (US sc).

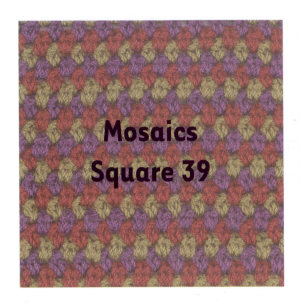

Mosaics
Square 39

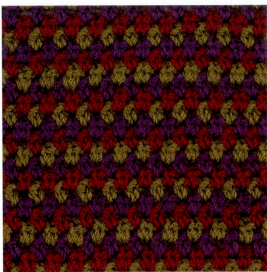

Colours A, B and D are required for this pattern.

With col A make 26 ch.

Row 1: (right side) cont with col A, htr (US hdc) in 3rd ch from hook, skip next ch, *2 htr (US hdc) in next ch, skip next ch, repeat from * across to last ch, htr (US hdc) in last ch, bringing in col B in last 3 loops of last st to complete last st, drop col A—25 htr (US hdc).

Row 2: cont with col B, 2 ch (count as htr [US hdc], beginning ch), turn, htr (US hdc) in same st, skip next 2 sts, *2 htr (US hdc) in next sp between next 2-htr (US hdc), skip next 2 sts, repeat from * across to last 2 sts, skip next st, htr (US hdc) in top of beginning ch, bringing in col D in last 3 loops to complete st, drop col B—25 htr (US hdc).

Row 3: cont with col D, repeat row 2, changing to col A—25 htr (US hdc).

Subsequent rows: repeat row 2, alternating colours as above: A-B-D-A, ending with col A.

Finishing: cont with col A, work the 2 rounds of edging for individual squares (see page 24) to complete the square.

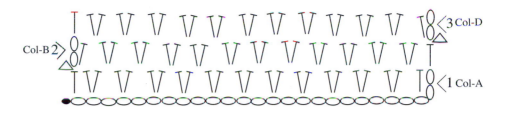

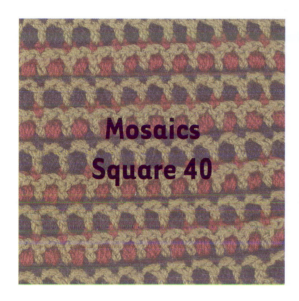
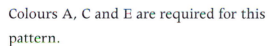

Colours A, C and E are required for this pattern.

With col A make 26 ch.

Row 1: cont with col A, dc (US sc) in 2nd ch from hook and in each ch across—25 dc (US sc).

Row 2: (right side) cont col A, 3 ch (count as tr [US dc], beginning ch), *tr (US dc) in next st, 1 ch, skip next st,

repeat from * across, tr (US dc) in last st, drop col A—11 x 1-ch sps.

Row 3: do not turn, remove hook, reinsert into top of beginning ch of same row and bring in col E, 1 ch, dc (US sc) in same st, dc (US sc) in next st, *working behind next 1-ch sp work cluster in skipped st 2 rows below, dc (US sc) in next st on working row, repeat from * across, dc (US sc) in last 2 sts, bringing in col A in last 2 loops of last st to complete st, finish off col E—11 x clusters.

Row 4: cont with col A, 3 ch, *tr (US dc) in next st, 1 ch, skip cluster, repeat from * across, tr (US dc) in last 2 sts, bringing in col B in last 2 loops of last st to complete st, drop col A—11 x 1-ch sps.

Row 5: cont with col B, 1 ch, dc (US sc) in same st, *dc (US sc) in next st, working behind next 1-ch sp work cluster in closing loop of skipped cluster 2 rows below, repeat from * across, dc (US sc) in last st, finish off col B—11 x clusters.

Row 6: do not turn, remove hook, reinsert in first st of same row and bring in col A, 3 ch, *tr (US dc) in next st, 1 ch, skip cluster, repeat from * across, tr (US dc) in last 2 sts—11 x 1-ch sps.

Subsequent rows: repeat rows 3 to 6, alternating colours and turning work as required, ending with row 3 with col E, bringing in col A in last 2 loops of last st to complete st, finish off col E—11 x clusters, then work a last row as follows.

Last row: cont with col A, 1 ch, turn, dc (US sc) same st and in each st across, finish off—25 dc (US sc).

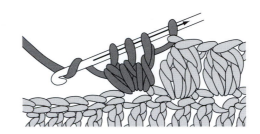

Cluster: (YO, insert hook in stitch indicated and draw up a loop, YO and draw through 2 loops on hook) 3 times, YO and draw through all 4 loops on hook—cluster made.

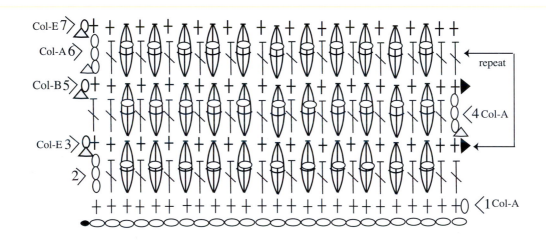

CLUSTERS AND BOBBLES

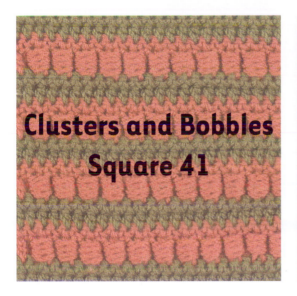

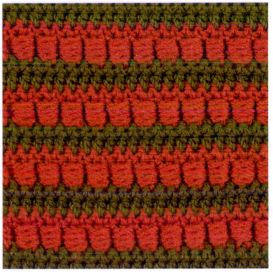

Colours A and C are required for this pattern.

With col A make 26 ch.

Row 1: (right side) cont with col A, htr (US hdc) in 3rd ch from hook and in each ch across—25 htr (US hdc).

Row 2: cont with col A, 1 ch, turn, dc (US sc) in first and in each st across to last 2 loops of last st, bringing in col C in last 2 loops to complete st, drop Col A—25 dc (US sc).

Row 3: cont with col C, 3 ch (count as tr [US dc]), turn, tr (US dc) in next st, work pineapple st across to last st, tr (US dc) in last st—11 pineapples.

Row 4: cont with col C, repeat row 2, changing to col A—25 dc (US sc).

Row 5: cont with col A, 2 ch, turn, htr (US hdc) in next st and each st across—25 htr (US hdc).

Row 6: cont with col A, repeat row 2 changing to col C—25 dc (US sc).

Subsequent rows: repeat rows 2 to 5, alternating colours A and C as above, ending with row 6, col A.

Pineapple stitch: tr (US dc) in next st, [YO, working around tr (US dc) just made insert hook from front to back and draw up a loop] 4 times, insert hook into next st, YO and draw through st and 9 loops on hook, 1 ch—pineapple st made.

Note: When working next pineapple st, work around tr (US dc) just made and back thread of previous pineapple.

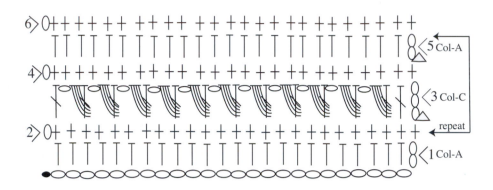

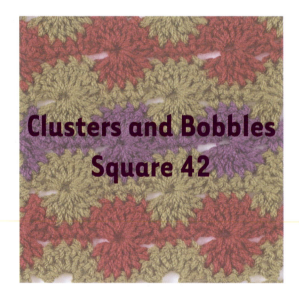

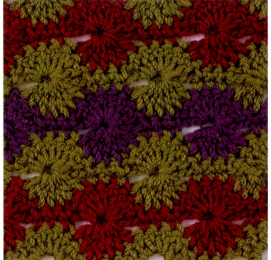

Colours A, B and D are required for this pattern.

With col A make 26 ch.

Row 1: cont with col A, dc (US sc) in 2nd ch from hook, *skip 3 ch, 7 tr (US dc) in next ch, skip 3 ch, dc (US sc) in next 3 ch, repeat from * across to last 4 ch, skip 3 ch, 4 tr (US dc) into last ch, bringing in col B in last 2 loops of last st to complete st, drop col A—25 sts.

Row 2: (right side) cont with col B, 1 ch, turn, dc (US sc) in first 2 sts, *3 ch, work cluster st over the next 7 sts, 3 ch, dc

(US sc) in next 3 sts, repeat from * across to last 3 sts, 3 ch, work cluster st over last 3 sts—25 sts.

Row 3: cont with col B, 3 ch (count as tr [US dc], beginning ch), turn, 2 tr (US dc) in same st, *skip 3 ch., dc (US sc) in next 3 sts, skip 3 ch, work 7 tr (US dc) in closing loop of next cluster st, repeat from * across to last 5 sts, skip 3 ch, dc (US sc) in last 2 sts, bringing in col A in last 2 loops of last st to complete st, finish off col B—25 sts.

Row 4: cont with col A, 3 ch, turn, work cluster st over next 3 sts, *3 ch, dc (US sc) in next 3 sts, 3 ch, work cluster st over next 7 sts, repeat from * across to last st, 3 ch, dc (US sc) in top of beginning ch—25 sts.

Row 5: cont with col A, 1 ch, turn, dc (US sc) in first st, *skip 3 ch, work 7 tr (US dc) in closing loop of next cluster st, dc (US sc) in next 3 sts, repeat from * across to last 4 sts, skip 3 ch, 4 tr (US dc) into top of beginning ch, bringing in col D in last 2 loops of last st to complete st, drop col A—25 sts.

Subsequent rows: repeat rows 2 to 5, alternating colours in the sequence A-B-A-D, ending with row 4, col A.

Cluster stitch: (YO, insert hook in st indicated and draw up a loop, YO and draw through 2 loops) repeat over number of sts indicated, YO and draw through all loops on hook, 1 ch to close—cluster st made.

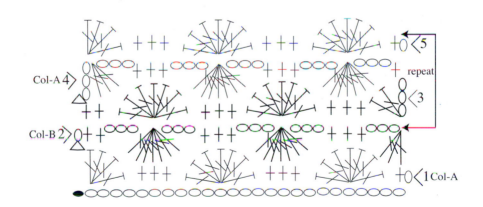

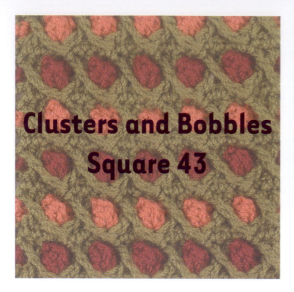

Clusters and Bobbles
Square 43

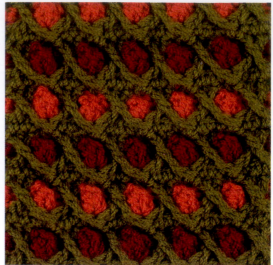

Colours A, B and C are required for this pattern.

With col A make 26 ch.

Row 1: (right side) cont col A, dc (US sc) in 2nd ch from hook and in each ch across—25 dc (US sc).

Row 2: cont with col A, 2 ch [count as htr (US hdc)], turn, htr (US hdc) in next st and in each st across to last 3 loops of last st, bringing in col B in last 3 loops to complete st—25 htr (US hdc).

Row 3: cont with col B, 1 ch, turn, dc (US sc) in first 4 sts, *work popcorn in next st, dc (US sc) in next 3 sts, repeat from * across, dc (US sc) in last st—5 x popcorns.

Row 4: cont with col B, 1 ch, turn, dc (US sc) in first st and in each st across to last 2 loops of last st, bringing in col A

in last 2 loops to complete st, finish off col B—25 dc (US sc).

Row 5: (skip unused st behind FPdtr [US tr]) cont with col A, 1 ch, turn, dc (US sc) in first st, work FPdtr (US tr) around post of st 4 sts forward 3 rows below htr (US hdc) directly under popcorn, dc (US sc) in next st on working row, work FPdtr (US tr) around st 2 sts backward 3 rows below, dc (US sc) in next st on working row, *work FPdtr (US tr) around post of st 4 sts forward 3 rows below, dc (US sc) in next st on working row, work FPdtr (US tr) around st 3 sts backward 3 rows below (in same st as first FPdtr [US tr] directly under popcorn), dc (US sc) in next st on working row, repeat from * across to last 4 sts, work FPdtr (US tr) around post of st 2 sts forward 3 rows below, dc (US sc) in next st on working row, work FPdtr (US tr) around post of st 3 sts backward 3 rows below—12 x FPdtr (US tr).

Row 6: cont with col A, repeat row 2, bringing in col C in last 3 loops of last st to complete st—25 htr (US hdc).

Subsequent rows: repeat rows 3 to 6, alternating colours B and C on rows 3 and 4, ending with row 6, col A, and a last row as follows.

Last row: cont with col A, 1 ch, turn, dc (US sc) in first and in each st across—25 dc (US sc).

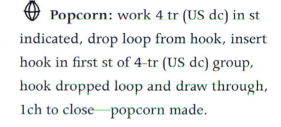 **Popcorn:** work 4 tr (US dc) in st indicated, drop loop from hook, insert hook in first st of 4-tr (US dc) group, hook dropped loop and draw through, 1ch to close—popcorn made.

Front post double treble (US front post treble): YO twice, insert hook from front to back around post of stitch indicated, (YO and draw through 2 loops) 3 times—FPdtr (US FPtr) made.

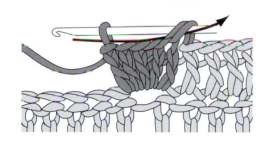

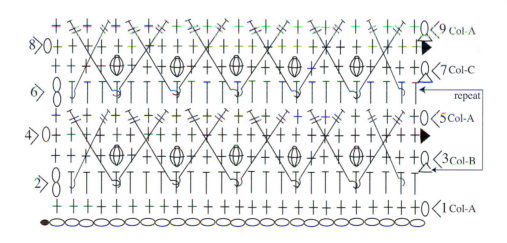

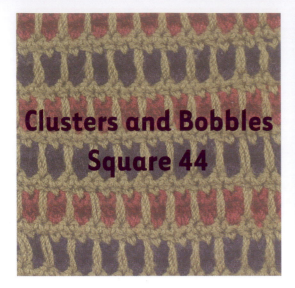

Clusters and Bobbles Square 44

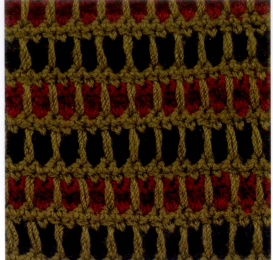

Colours A, B and E are required for this pattern.

With col A make 26 ch.

Row 1: (right side) cont col A, dc (US sc) in 2nd ch from hook and in each ch across—25 dc (US sc).

Row 2: cont with col A, 1 ch, turn, dc (US sc) in first st and in each st across to last 2 loops of last st, bringing in col E in last 2 loops to complete st, drop col A—25 dc (US sc).

Row 3: cont with col E, 3 ch (count as htr +1 ch), turn, skip next st, *work cluster in next st, 1 ch, skip next st, repeat from * across, htr in last st—11 x clusters.

Row 4: cont with col E, 1 ch, turn, dc (US sc) in first st, and in each 1-ch sp and cluster across to last 2 loops of

last st, bringing in col A in last 2 loops to complete st, finish off col E—25 dc (US sc).

Row 5: cont with col A, 1 ch, turn, dc (US sc) in first st, *work Ltr (US Ldc) in skipped st directly 3 rows below, dc (US sc) in next st, repeat from * across—12 Ltr (US Ldc).

Row 6: cont with col A, repeat row 2, changing to col B, drop col A—25 dc.

Subsequent rows: repeat rows 3 to 6, alternating colours in the sequence A-E-A-B, ending with row 6, col A, finish off.

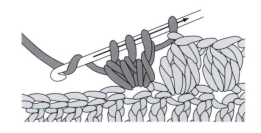

Cluster stitch: (YO, insert hook in st indicated and draw up a loop, YO and draw through 2 loops) 3 times, YO and draw through all 4 loops on hook, 1 ch to close—cluster st made.

Long treble (US long double crochet): YO, insert hook into st indicated and draw up a long loop even with st on working row, (YO and draw through 2 loops) twice—Ltr (US Ldc) made.

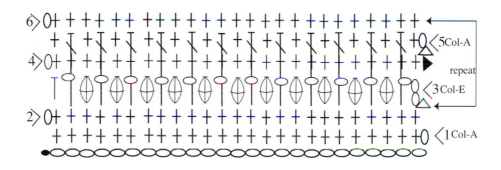

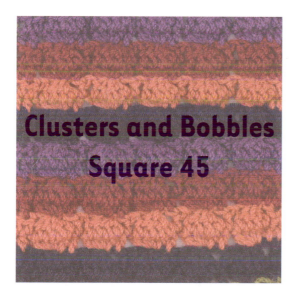

Colours A, B, C, D and E are required for this pattern.

This is a wide pattern; work tightly or use a smaller hook to stay in line with other 63 squares.

With col A make 26 ch.

Row 1: cont col A, dc (US sc) in 2nd ch from hook and in each ch across to last

2 loops of last st, bringing in col E in last 2 loops to complete st, finish off col A—25 dc (US sc).

Row 2: (right side) cont with col E, 2 ch (count as htr [US hdc]), turn, htr (US hdc) in next 2 sts, 1 ch, skip next st, *4 htr (US hdc) in next st, 1 ch, skip next st, htr (US hdc) in next st, 1 ch, repeat from * across, htr (US hdc) in last 3 sts—5 x shells.

Row 3: cont with col E, 2 ch, turn, htr (US hdc) in next 2 sts, 1 ch, skip next 1-ch sp, *work cluster over next 4 sts, 1 ch, skip next 1-ch sp, htr (US hdc) in next st, 1 ch, skip next 1-ch sp, repeat from * across to last 3 sts, 1 ch, skip next 1-ch sp, htr (US hdc) in each last 3 sts, bringing in col C in last 3 loops of last st to complete st, finish off col E—5 x clusters.

Row 4: cont with col C, 2 ch, turn, htr (US hdc) in next 2 sts, 1 ch, skip next 1-ch sp, *work 4 htr (US hdc) in closing loop of next cluster, 1 ch, skip next 1-ch sp, htr (US hdc) in next st, 1 ch, skip next 1-ch sp, repeat from * across, htr (US hdc) in last 3 sts—5 x shells.

Row 5: cont with col C, repeat row 3, changing to col D, finish off col C—5 x clusters.

Subsequent rows: repeat rows 4 and 5, alternating colours in the sequence E-C-D-B, ending with row 5, changing to col A in last 3 loops of last st and working a last row as follows.

Last row: cont with col A, 1 ch, turn, dc (US sc) in each st and 1-ch sp across, finish off—25 dc (US sc).

Cluster stitch: (YO, insert hook in st indicated and draw up a loop, YO and draw through 2 loops) repeat over number of sts indicated, YO and draw through all loops on hook—cluster st made.

Cluster stitch: (YO, insert hook in st indicated and draw up a loop, YO and draw through 2 loops) repeat over number of sts indicated, YO and draw through all loops on hook—cluster st made.

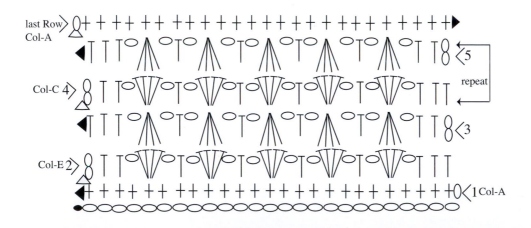

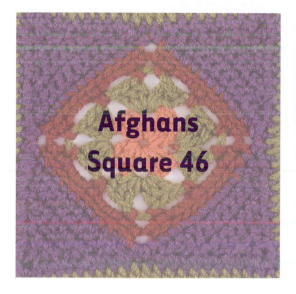

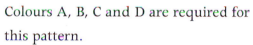

Colours A, B, C and D are required for this pattern.

With col C make 4 ch, join with ss to form a ring.

Round 1: cont with col C, 3 ch (count as tr [US dc], beginning ch), into ring work 2 tr (US dc), 2 ch, (3 tr [US dc], 2 ch) 3 times, join with ss to top of beginning ch, finish off—4 x shell + 4 x 2-ch sps.

Round 2: join col A with ss in any 2-ch sp, (3 ch, 2 tr [US dc], 3 ch, 3 tr [US dc]) in same sp, 1 ch, (3 tr [US dc], 3 ch, 3 tr [US dc], 1 ch) in each 2-ch sp around, join with ss to top of beginning ch, finish off—8 shells + 4 x 3 ch sps.

Round 3: join col B with dc (US sc) in any corner 3-ch sp, 3 ch, dc (US sc) in same sp, 3 ch, dc (US sc) in next 1-ch sp, 3 ch, *(dc [US sc], 3 ch, dc [US sc]) in next corner sp, 3 ch, dc (US sc) in next 1 ch sp, 3 ch, repeat from * around, join with ss in first dc (US sc), do not finish off—12 dc (US sc) + 12 x 3 ch sps.

Round 4: cont with col B, ss into next corner sp, 1 ch, (dc [US sc], 3 ch, dc [US sc]) in same sp, dc (US sc) in next st, 3 dc (US sc) in next 3 ch sp, dc (US sc) in next st, 3 dc (US sc) in next 3-ch sp, dc (US sc) in next st, *(dc [US sc], 3 ch, dc [US sc]) in corner sp, dc (US sc) in next st, 3 dc (US sc) in next 3-ch sp, dc (US sc) in next st, 3 dc (US sc) in next 3-ch sp, dc (US sc) in next st, repeat from * around, join with ss in first dc (US sc), finish off—count 11 dc (US sc) between each corner.

Row 5: from now on you will be working in *rows*, turning, decreasing and creating 4 triangles that radiate outward from your work (count 13 dc [US sc] first row) with col D:

5a: join with dc (US sc) (on left) of any corner sp, working in back loops only dc (US sc) in each dc (US sc) across, dc (US sc) in next corner sp—13 dc (US sc);

5b: 1 ch, turn, from now on working in both loops decrease next 2 dc (US sc), dc (US sc) in each dc (US sc) across to last 2 dc (US sc), decrease last 2 dc (US sc), continue in this way until 3 dc (US sc) remain;

5c: decrease first 2 dc (US sc), 2 ch, decrease 2nd and 3rd dc (US sc) (i.e. use 2nd dc [US sc] twice), finish off, 2-ch sp at point, place marker in 2-ch point;

5d: repeat a, b and c for each corner in col D to last corner, do not finish off last corner.

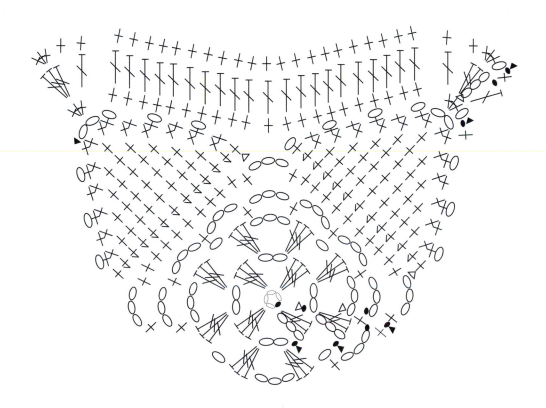

Round 6: when all triangles are complete you will be working between triangle corner tips around turn to wrong side, ss into last dc (US sc) dec of previous row and into 2-ch point, 1 ch, *3 dc (US sc) in corner point, work 21 dc (US sc) evenly placed across to next 2-ch corner, repeat from * around, join with ss to first dc (US sc), finish off, count 23 dc (US sc) between corner sts—96 dc (US sc).

Round 7: with right side facing, join col A with ss in any corner dc (US sc), 3 ch, 2 tr (US dc) in same st, tr (US dc) in each dc (US sc) across to next corner dc (US sc), *3 tr (US dc) in corner dc (US sc), tr (US dc) in each dc (US sc) across to next corner dc (US sc), repeat from * around, join with ss to top of beginning ch, do not finish off, count 25 tr (US dc) between corner sts—104 tr (US dc).

Round 8: 1 ch, dc (US sc) in same st, *dc (US sc) in each tr (US dc) across to corner tr (US dc), 3 dc (US sc) in corner tr (US dc), repeat from * around, join with ss to first dc (US sc), finish off, count 27 dc (US sc) between corner sts—112 dc (US sc).

⋏ **dc decrease:** insert hook into first st and draw up a loop, insert hook into next st and draw up a loop, YO and draw through 3 loops on hoop.

✝ Work in back loops.

> **Joining with dc:** begin with a slip knot on hook. Insert hook into stitch or space indicated, YO and pull up loop, YO and draw through both loops on hook.

Colours A, B, C, D and E are required for this pattern.

With col D make 3 ch, join with ss to form a ring.

Round 1: cont with col D, 1 ch, *dc (US sc) into ring, make 4 ch then dc (US sc) in 2nd ch from hook and in each next 2 ch, repeat from * 4 times more, join with ss to first dc (US sc), finish off col D—5 points.

Round 2: join col A with ss in top st of any point, *skip next 3 sts, (dtr [US tr], tr [US dc], dtr [US tr]) in next st (on round 1), ss in top of next point, repeat from * around, join with ss in first ss, finish off col A—10 x dtr (US tr) + 5 x tr (US dc) + 5 x ss.

Round 3: join col B with ss in any ss, *skip next st, (htr [US hdc], tr [US dc], dtr [US tr], 1 ch, dtr [US tr], tr [US dc], htr [US hdc]) in next st, skip next st, ss

in next ss, repeat from * around, join with ss in first ss, finish off col B—10 x dtr (US tr) + 10 x tr (US dc) + 5 x ss + 5 x 1-ch point.

Round 4: join col E with ss in back loop of any 1-ch point, *skip next 3 sts, (dtr [US tr],3 tr [US dc], dtr [US tr]) in next st, skip next 3 sts, ss in back loop of next 1-ch point, repeat from * around, join with ss in first ss, finish off col E—30 sts.

Round 5: join col C with dc (US sc) in any st, dc (US sc) in same st, 2 dc (US sc) in each st around, join with ss to first dc (US sc), finish off col C—60 dc (US sc).

Round 6: join col D with ss in dc (US sc) above 2nd tr (US dc) of any tr (US dc) group of round 4, 6 ch (count as dtr [US tr] + 2 ch), dtr (US tr) in next st, *tr (US dc) in next st, htr (US hdc) in next 2 sts, **dc (US sc) in next 7 sts, htr (US hdc) in next 2 sts, tr (US dc) in next st**, dtr (US

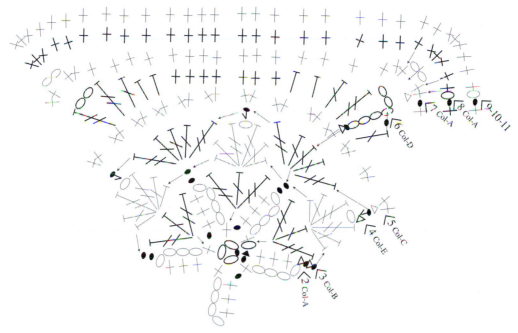

tr) in next st, 2 ch, dtr (US tr) in next st, repeat from * around to last 10 sts, repeat from ** to ** once, then join with ss to 4th ch of beginning ch, finish off col D—4 x 2-ch sps + 8 x dtr (US tr) + 8 x tr (US dc) + 16 x htr (US hdc) + 28 x dc (US sc).

Round 7: join col A with dc (US sc) in any 2-ch sp, (dc [US sc], 2 ch, 2 dc [US sc]) in same sp, *working in back loops only dc (US sc) in each st across to next 2-ch sp, (2 dc [US sc], 2ch, 2 dc [US sc]) in 2-ch sp, repeat from * around, join with ss to first dc (US sc), do not finish off, count 19 dc (US sc) between corner 2-ch sps.

Round 8: cont with col A, 1 ch, dc (US sc) in same st, *dc (US sc) in each st to corner 2-ch sp, 3 dc (US sc) in corner 2-ch sp, repeat from * around, join with ss to first dc (US sc), do not finish off,

count 21 dc (US sc) between corner sts.

Round 9: cont with col A, 1 ch, dc (US sc) in same st, *dc (US sc) in each st to corner st, 3 dc (US sc) in corner st, repeat from * around, join with ss to first dc (US sc), do not finish off, count 23 dc (US sc) between corner sts.

Round 10: repeat round 9, do not finish off, count 25 dc (US sc) between corner sts.

Round 11: repeat round 9, finish off, count 27 dc (US sc) between corner sts.

⌡ Slip stitch in back loops.

Joining with dc: begin with a slip knot on hook. Insert hook into stitch or space indicated, YO and pull up loop, YO and draw through both loops on hook.

Colours A, B, C, D and E are required for this pattern.

With col C make 4 ch, join with ss to form a ring.

Round 1: cont with col C, into ring work beginning popcorn, 3 ch, and (popcorn, 3 ch) 3 times, join with ss to top of beginning popcorn, finish off col C—4 x popcorns + 4 x 3-ch sps.

Round 2: join col D with ss in any 3-ch sp, 3 ch (count as tr [US dc], beginning ch), (2 tr [US dc], 2 ch, 3 tr [US dc]) in same sp, 1 ch, (3 tr [US dc], 2 ch, 3 tr [US dc], 1 ch) in each 3-ch sp around, join with ss to top of beginning ch, finish off col D—8 shells + 4 x 2-ch sps + 4 x 1-ch sps.

Round 3: join col B with ss in any corner 2-ch sp, work (beginning popcorn, 3 ch, popcorn) in same sp,

*3 ch, popcorn in next 1-ch sp, 3 ch, (popcorn, 3 ch) twice in next 2-ch sp, repeat from * around, join with ss to top of beginning popcorn, finish off col B—12 popcorns + 12 x 3-ch sps.

Round 4: join col E with ss into any corner 3-ch sp, 3 ch, (2 tr [US dc], 2 ch, 3 tr [US dc]) in same sp, *1 ch, (3 tr [US dc] in next 3-ch sp, 1 ch) twice, (3 tr [US dc], 2 ch, 3 tr [US dc]) in next corner 3-ch sp, repeat from * around, join with ss to top of beginning ch, finish off col E—48 tr (US dc) + 4 x 2-ch sps + 12 x 1-ch sps.

Row 5: From now on you will be working in *rows*, turning, decreasing and creating 4 triangles that radiate outward from your work (count 17 dc [US sc] first row):

5a: with col B, join with dc (US sc) in 2nd ch of any corner 2-ch sp, working in back loops only, dc (US sc) in each dc (US sc) across, dc (US sc) in next corner ch—17 dc (US sc);

5b: 1 ch, turn, from now on work in both loops, decrease next 2 dc (US sc), dc (US sc) in each dc (US sc) across to last 2 dc (US sc), decrease last 2 dc (US sc), continue in this way until 3 dc (US sc) remain;

5c: 1 ch, turn, decrease first 2 dc (US sc), 2 ch, decrease 2nd and 3rd dc (US sc) (i.e. use 2nd dc [US sc] twice), finish off col B, 2-ch sp at point, place marker in 2-ch point;

5d: repeat a, b and c for each corner in col B.

Round 6: when all triangles are complete you will be working between triangle corner points around (count 27 dc [US sc] between corner sts) with right side facing, join col A with ss in any corner 2-ch point, 3 ch, 2 tr (US dc)

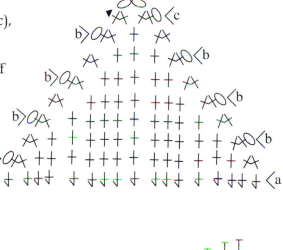

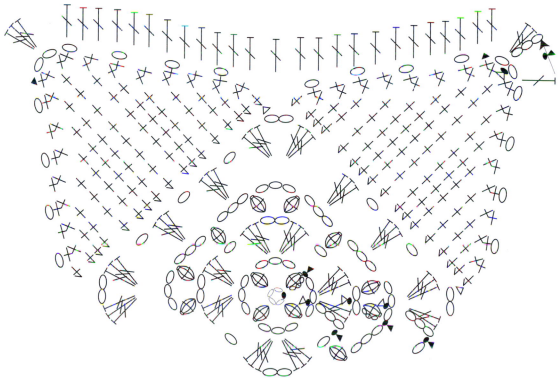

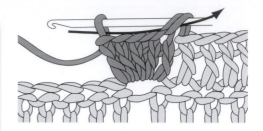

in same sp, *work 25 tr (US dc) evenly across to next 2-ch point, 3 tr (US dc) in next 2-ch point repeat from * around, join with ss top of beginning, finish off—112 dc (US sc).

Beginning popcorn: 3 ch, 3 tr (US dc) in st/sp indicated, remove hook and insert in top of first 3 ch, pick up dropped loop and draw through loop on hook—beginning popcorn made.

Popcorn: 4 tr (US dc) in st/sp indicated, remove hook and insert in first tr (US dc) of 4-tr (US dc) group, pick up dropped loop and draw through loop on hook—popcorn made.

dc decrease: insert hook into first st and draw up a loop, insert hook into next st and draw up a loop, YO and draw through 3 loops on hoop.

Work in back loops.

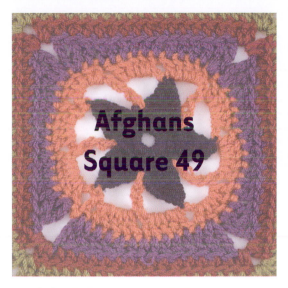

Colours A, B, C, D and E are required for this pattern.

With col E make 5 ch, join with ss to form a ring.

Round 1: cont col E, 1 ch, into ring work 16 dc (US sc), join with ss to first dc (US sc), do not finish off—16 dc (US sc).

Round 2: cont with col E, *5 ch, dc (US sc) in 2nd ch from hook, htr (US hdc) in next ch, tr (US dc) in next ch, dtr (US tr) in next ch, skip 2 sts, ss into next st, repeat from * around, join with ss in beginning st, finish off col E—5 x points.

Round 3: join col C with ss in top of any point, *5 ch, skip next 4 sts, dtr (US tr) in next ss (on round 2), 5 ch, ss in top of next point, repeat from * around, join with ss to first ss, do not finish off—5 x

dtr (US tr) + 10 x 5-ch sps.

Round 4: cont col C, ss into next 5-ch sp, 3 ch [count as tr (US dc), beginning ch], 5 tr (US dc) in same sp, 5 tr (US dc) in next 8 5-ch sps, 6 tr (US dc) in last 5-ch sp, join with ss in top of beginning ch, finish off col C—52 tr (US dc).

Round 5: join col D with ss in last st on round 4, 4 ch (count as dtr [US tr]), dtr (US tr) in same st, *tr (US dc) in next 4 sts, htr (US hdc) in next 3 sts, tr (US dc) in next 4 sts, 2 dtr (US tr) in next st, 2 ch, 2 dtr (US tr) in next st, repeat from * around, ending with 2 dtr (US tr) in last st, 2 ch, join with ss to top of beginning 4-ch, finish off col D—60 sts.

Round 6: join col B with ss in any 2-ch sp, 2 ch (count as htr [US hdc]), (htr [US hdc], 2 ch, 2 htr [US hdc]) in same sp, working in back loops only, *htr (US hdc) in each st across to next 2-ch sp,

(2 htr [US hdc], 2 ch, 2 htr [US hdc]) in 2-ch sp, repeat from * around, join with ss to top of beginning 2-ch, finish off col B, count 19 htr (US hdc) between 2-ch sps.

Round 7: with col A repeat round 6, do not finish off, count 23 htr (US hdc) between 2-ch sp.

Round 8: cont with col A and working in both loops from now on, 1 ch, dc (US sc) in same st, *dc (US sc) each st across to next corner 2-ch sp, 3 dc (US sc) in 2-ch sp, repeat from * around, join with ss in first dc (US sc), do not finish off, count 25 dc (US sc) between corner sts.

Round 9: cont with col A, 1 ch, dc (US sc) in same st, *dc (US sc) each st across to next corner 2-ch sp, 3 dc (US sc) in corner st, repeat from * around, join with ss to first dc (US sc), finish off, count 27 dc (US sc) between corner sts—112 total dc (US sc) around.

Ʇ Work in back loops.

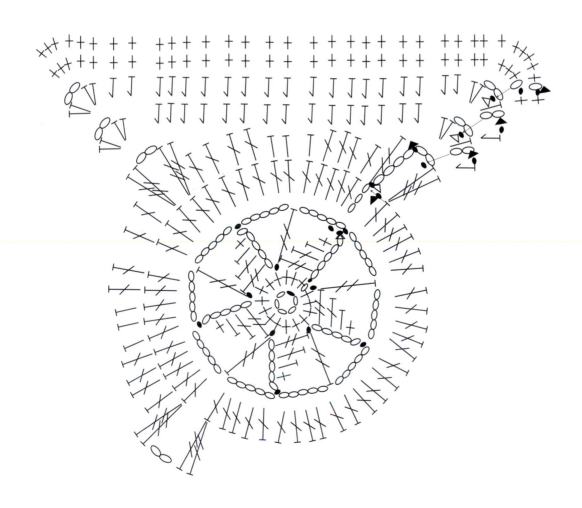

Colours A, B, C and D are required for this pattern.

With col B make 4 ch, join with ss to form a ring.

Round 1: cont col B, 3 ch [count as tr (US dc), beginning ch], into ring work 11 tr (US dc), join with ss to top of beginning ch, finish off Col B—12 tr (US dc).

Round 2: join col D with ss in finishing st of previous round, 3 ch, tr (US dc) in same st, 2 tr (US dc) in each next 2 sts, 1 ch, *2 tr (US dc) in each next 3 sts, 1 ch, repeat from * around, join with ss in top of beginning ch, finish off col D—24 tr (US dc) + 4 x 1-ch sps.

Round 3: join col C with ss in finishing st of previous round, 3 ch, tr (US dc) in same st, 2 tr (US dc) in next st, tr (US dc) dec over next 2 sts, 2 tr (US dc) in each

next 2 sts, 2 ch, *2 tr (US dc) in each next 2 sts, tr (US dc) dec over next 2 sts, 2 tr (US dc) in each next 2 sts, 2 ch, repeat from * around, join with ss to top of beginning ch, finish off col C—4 x tr (US dc) decs + 4 x 2-ch sps.

Round 4: (skip unused st behind FPTtr [US dtr]) join col B with ss in finishing st of previous round, 3 ch, tr (US dc) in same st, *tr (US dc) in each next 3 sts, work FPTtr (US dtr) around st directly below on round 1, tr (US dc) in each next 3 sts, 2 tr (US dc) in next st, 2ch, 2 tr (US dc) in next st, repeat from * around, join with ss to top of beginning ch, finish off col B—4 FPTtr (US dtr).

Round 5: join col D with ss in any 2-ch sp, work (beginning popcorn, 3 ch, popcorn) in same sp, *htr (US hdc) in each next 5 sts, work popcorn in next FPTtr (US dtr), htr (US hdc) in next 5 sts, work (popcorn, 3 ch, popcorn) in next 3-ch sp, repeat from * around, join with ss to top of beginning popcorn, do not finish off—12 x popcorns, count 13 sts between corner 3-ch sps.

Round 6: cont with col D, ss into next 3-ch sp, (2 ch [count as htr [US hdc]), popcorn, htr (US hdc) in same 3-ch sp, *htr (US hdc) in each st across to next 3-ch sp, [htr (US hdc), popcorn, htr (US hdc)] in 3-ch sp, repeat from * around, join with ss to top of beginning 2-ch, finish off col D, count 15 sts between corner popcorns.

Round 7: join col C with ss in any corner popcorn, [3 ch, tr (US dc), 2 ch, 2 tr (US dc)] in same st, *dc (US sc) in each st across to next corner popcorn, [2 tr (US dc), 2 ch, 2 tr (US dc)] in corner popcorn, repeat from * around, finish off col C, count 19 sts between 2-ch sps.

Round 8: join col B with dc (US sc) in any 2-ch sp, 2 dc (US sc) in same sp, *dc (US sc) in each st across to next 2-ch sp, 3 dc (US sc) in next 2-ch sp, repeat from * around, join with ss to first dc (US sc), finish off col B, count 21 sts between corner sts—88 total sts around.

Round 9: join col A with ss in any corner st, (2 ch [count as htr [US hdc], 2 htr [US hdc]) in same st, *htr (US hdc) in each st across to next corner st, 3 htr

(US hdc) in next corner st, repeat from * around, join with ss to top of beginning 2 ch, do not finish off, count 23 sts between corner sts—96 total dc (US sc) around.

Round 10: cont with col A, 1 ch, dc (US sc) in same st, *3 dc (US sc) in corner st, dc (US sc) in each st across to next corner st, repeat from * around, join with ss to first dc (US sc), do not finish off, count 25 sts between corner sts—104 total dc (US sc) around.

Round 11: cont with col A, 1 ch, dc (US sc) in same st, dc (US sc) in next st, *3 dc (US sc) in corner st, dc (US sc) in each st across to next corner st, repeat from * around, join with ss to first dc (US sc), finish off, count 27 sts between corner sts—112 total dc (US sc) around.

Treble decrease (US double crochet decrease): YO, insert hook into st indicated and draw up a loop, YO and draw through 2 loops on hook) twice YO and draw through 3 loops on hook—tr (US dc) dec made.

Joining with dc: begin with a slip knot on hook. Insert hook into stitch or space indicated, YO and pull up loop, YO and draw through both loops on hook.

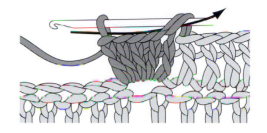

Front post triple treble (US front post double treble): YO 3 times, insert hook from front to back around post of stitch indicated, (YO and draw through 2 loops) 4 times—FPTtr (US FPdtr) made.

Beginning popcorn: 3 ch, 3 tr (US dc) in st/sp indicated, remove hook and insert in top of first 3 ch, pick up dropped loop and draw through loop on hook—beginning popcorn made.

Popcorn: 4 tr (US dc) in st/sp indicated, remove hook and insert in first tr (US dc) of 4-tr (US dc) group, pick up dropped loop and draw through loop on hook—popcorn made.

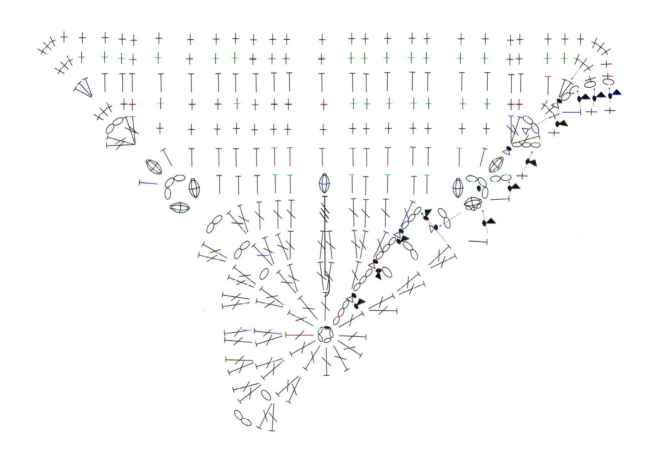

VARIABLE STRIPES

Variable Stripes
Square 51

Colours A, C and D are required for this pattern.

With col A make 27 ch.

Row 1: cont with col A, tr (US dc) into 4th ch from hook and in each ch across to last 2 loops of last st, bringing in col D in last 2 loops to complete st, drop col A—25 tr (US dc).

Row 2: (right side) cont with col D, 1 ch, turn, dc (US sc) in first st and in each st across to last 2 loops of last st, bringing in col C in last 2 loops to complete st, drop col D—25 dc (US sc).

Row 3: (keep cobble st to right side of work) cont with col C, 1 ch, turn, work one row of cobble st across to last st, dc (US sc) in last st—25 sts.

Row 4: cont with col C, 1 ch, turn, dc (US sc) in first and in each st across to last 2 loops of last st, bringing in col D in last 2 loops to complete st, finish off col C.

Row 5: cont with col D, 1 ch, turn, dc (US sc) in first and in each st across to last 2 loops of last st, bringing in Ccol A in last 2 loops to complete st, finish off col D—25 dc (US sc).

Row 6: cont with col A, 3 ch, turn tr (US dc) in next and in each st across to last 2 loops of last st, bringing in col D in last 2 loops to complete st, drop col A—25 tr (US dc).

Subsequent rows: repeat rows 2 to 6, alternating colours as above (A-D-C-D-A), ending with row 6, col A.

Cobble stitch: *dc (US sc) in first st, dtr (US tr) in next st, repeat from *

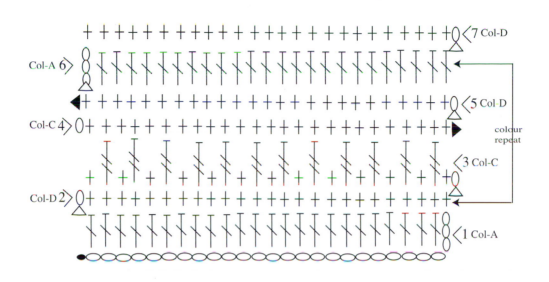

Variable Stripes Square 52

Colours A and D are required for this pattern.

With col A make 27 ch.

Row 1: (right side) cont with col A, tr (US dc) in 4th ch from hook and in each ch across to last 2 loops of last st, bringing in col D in last 2 loops to complete st, drop col A—25 tr (US dc).

Row 2: cont with col D, 1 ch (count as ss), turn, *tr (US dc) next st, ss in next st, repeat from * across, drop col D—13 ss +12 tr (US dc).

Row 3: do not turn, remove hook, reinsert into ss at beginning of same row and bring in col A, 3 ch (count as tr [US dc]), tr (US dc) in next and in each st across to last 2 loops of last st, bringing in col D in last 2 loops to complete st, drop col A—25 tr (US dc).

Row 4: cont col D, 1 ch, turn, dc (US sc) in first st and in each st across, drop col D—25 dc (US sc).

Row 5: do not turn, remove hook, reinsert hook into st at beginning of same row and bring in col A, 3 ch, tr (US dc) in next st and in each st across to last 2 loops of last st, bringing in col D in last 2 loops to complete st, drop col A—25 tr (US dc).

Subsequent rows: repeat rows 2 to 5, ending with col A.

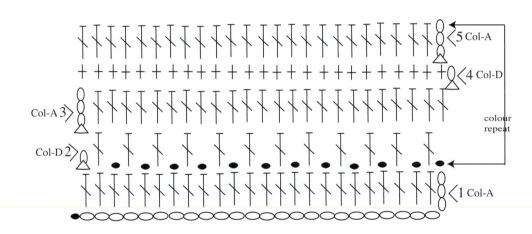

Colours A, B, C, D and E are required for this pattern.

With col A make 27 ch.

Row 1: (right side) cont with col A, tr (US dc) into 4th ch from hook and in each ch across—25 tr (US dc).

Row 2: cont with col A, 3 ch [count as tr (US dc)], turn, working in front loops only tr (US dc) in next st and in each st across—25 tr (US dc).

Row 3: cont with col A, 3 ch, turn, working in back loops only tr (US dc) in next st and in each st across—25 tr (US dc).

Subsequent rows: repeat rows 2 and 3 to desired size.

When square is desired size, finish off, then work crab stitch surface

embellishment in unused loops as follows, being guided by diagram and photograph.

Crab stitch surface embellishment: with right side facing work crab st in unused loops on each row in the colour sequence E-B-D-C.

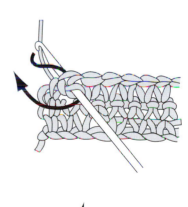

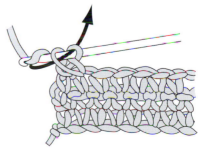

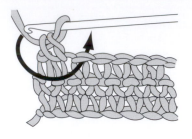

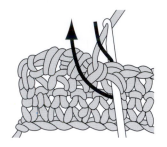

Crab stitch: reverse dc (US sc) always worked on right side and in the opposite direction as usual—join as required, 1 ch, *insert hook into the next st on right, YO and draw up a loop, YO and draw through both loops on hook, repeat from * across—crab st made.

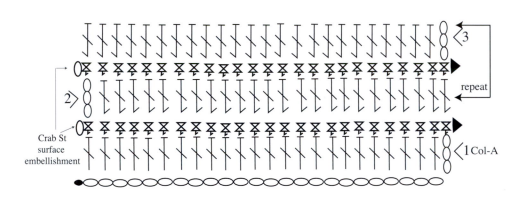

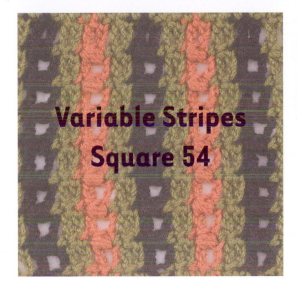

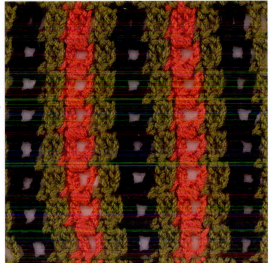

Colours A, C and E are required for this pattern.

With col A make 26 ch.

Row 1: (right side) cont with col A, dc (US sc) in 2nd ch from hook and in each ch across—25 dc (US sc).

Row 2: cont with col A, 1 ch, turn, dc (US sc) in first st, *2 ch, skip 2 sts, dc (US sc) in next st, repeat from * across to last 2 loops of last st, bringing in col E in last 2 loops to complete st, drop col A—8 x 2-ch sps + 9 x dc (US sc).

Row 3: cont with col E, 1 ch, turn, dc (US sc) in first st, *2 ch, skip next 2-ch sp, dc (US sc) in next st, repeat from * across—8 x 2-ch sps + 9 x dc (US sc).

Row 4: cont with col E, 1 ch, turn, dc (US sc) in first st, *2 ch, skip next 2-ch

sp, work short puff st in next st, repeat from * to last st, dc (US sc) in last st, bringing in col A in last 2 loops of last st to complete st, drop col E—7 x short puff sts + 8 x 2-ch sps.

Row 5: cont with col A, repeat row 3.

Row 6: cont with col A, repeat row 2, changing to col C.

Row 7: cont with col C, repeat row 3.

Row 8: cont with col C, repeat row 4, changing to col A.

Subsequent rows: repeat rows 2 to 6, ending with row 2 in col A and working a last row as follows.

Last row: cont with col A, 1 ch, turn, dc (US sc) in first st, 2 dc (US sc) in next 2-ch sp, *dc (US sc) in next st, 2 dc (US sc) in next 2-ch sp, repeat from * across to last st, dc (US sc) in last st, finish off—25 dc (US sc).

Short puff stitch: insert hook into st indicated, YO and draw up a loop, (YO, insert hook into same st and draw up a loop) twice, YO and draw through all 6 loops on hook, 1 ch to close—short puff st made.

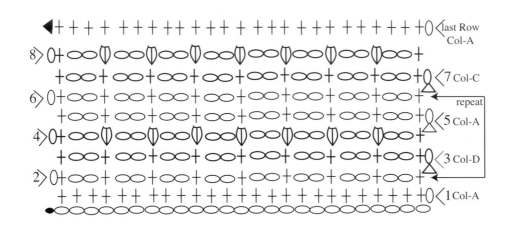

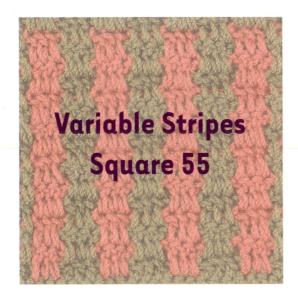

Variable Stripes Square 55

Colours A and C are required for this pattern.

With col A make 26 ch.

Row 1: cont with col A, dc (US sc) in 2nd ch from hook and in each ch across—25 dc (US sc).

Row 2: (right side) cont with col A, 3 ch (count as tr (US dc), beginning ch), turn, tr (US dc) in next st, *3 ch, skip next 3 sts, tr (US dc) in next 3 sts, repeat from * across, tr (US dc) in each last 2 sts, bringing in col C in last 2 loops of last st to complete st, drop col A—4 x 3-ch sps.

Row 3: cont with col C, 4 ch (count as tr [US dc], beginning ch + 1 ch), turn, skip next st, *working over 3-ch sp, work Ltr (US Ldc) into each 3 skipped sts of previous row, 3 ch, skip next 3 sts, repeat from * across to last 2 sts, 1 ch, skip next st, tr (US dc) in last st, drop col C—2 x 1-ch sps + 3 x 3-ch sps.

Row 4: do not turn, remove hook, reinsert in 3rd ch of beginning 4-ch and bring in col A, 3 ch, work Ltr (US Ldc) over next 1-ch sp in skipped st of previous row, *3 ch, skip next 3 sts, Ltr (US Ldc) in each next 3 skipped sts of previous row, repeat from * across to last 2 sts, work Ltr (US Ldc) over next 1-ch sp in skipped st of previous row, tr (US dc) in last st, bringing in col C in last 2 loops of last st to complete st, drop col A—4 x 3-ch sps.

Subsequent rows: repeat rows 3 and 4, alternating colours A and C as above and turning work as required, ending with row 4, col A, and a last row as follows.

Last row: cont with col A, 1 ch, turn, dc (US sc) in next 2 sts, *Ltr (US Ldc) into each 3 skipped sts of previous row, dc (US sc) in next 3 sts, repeat from * across, dc (US sc) in each last 2 sts, finish off—25 dc (US sc).

⟊ **Long treble (US long double crochet):** YO, insert hook into st indicated and draw up a long loop level with st on working row, (YO and draw through 2 loops) twice—Ltr (US Ldc) made.

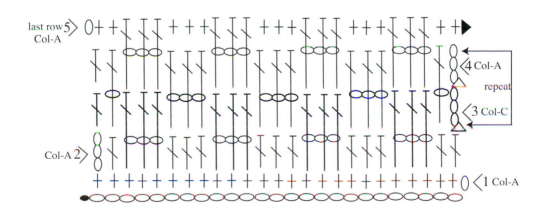

A QUICK BULLION TUTORIAL

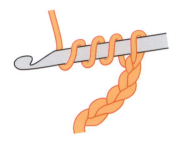

Step 1: make any number of ch plus 3, *wrap yarn around hook shaft 3 times—4 loops on hook.

Step 2: insert hook into 4th ch from hook and draw up a loop—5 loops on hook.

Step 3: draw this loop just made through the 3-wrapped-loops only—2 loops left on hook.

Drawing through all the wraps is the most difficult part when mastering bullions. You can either:

- ◣ draw through one wrapped loop at a time by using your left thumb to separate each loop on hook then slip your hook under each loop until 2 loops remain; or
- ◣ lift off each loop manually with your fingers until 2 loops remain.

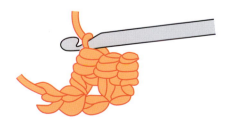

Step 4: YO and draw through both loops, 1 loop on hook—bullion made.

For subsequent bullions repeat from * in step 1, inserting hook into next ch.

NOVELTY SQUARES

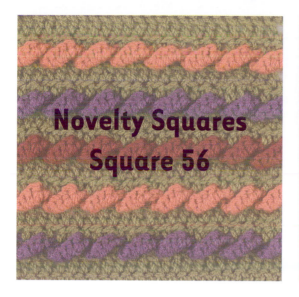

Colours A, B, C and D are required for this pattern.

With col A make 27 ch.

Row 1: cont with col A, tr (US dc) in 4th ch from hook and in each ch across—25 tr (US dc).

Row 2: (right side) cont with col A, 3 ch [count as tr (US dc), beginning ch], turn, tr (US dc) in next and in each st across, drop col A—25 tr (US dc).

Row 3: do not turn, remove hook and join col D with ss in top of beginning ch of same row, *3 ch, skip next 2 sts, ss in next st, turn to wrong side, work coil st, turn to right side and working behind coil st just made dc (US sc) in each 2 skipped sts, repeat from * across, finish

off col D—16 x dc (US sc) + 9 x ss + 8 x coil sts.

Row 4: do not turn, remove hook, reinsert in last ss of previous row and bring in col A, 3 ch, turn, *htr (US hdc) in next 2 sts, tr (US dc) in next ss, repeat from * across—9 x tr (US dc) + 16 x htr (US hdc).

Row 5: cont with col A, repeat row 2—25 tr (US dc).

Subsequent rows: repeat rows 3 to 5, alternating colours in the sequence A-D-A-C-A-B-A-D-A-C and turning work as required, ending with row 2, col A, finish off.

Coil stitch: with wrong side facing, work 5 dc (US sc) over 3-ch loop—coil st made.

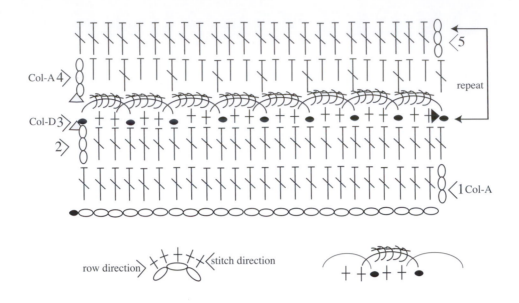

Col-A 4
Col-D 3
2
5
repeat
1 Col-A

row direction > stitch direction

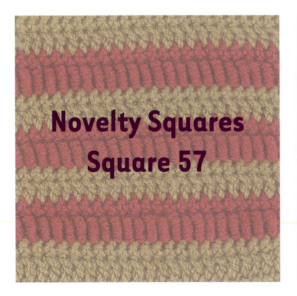

Novelty Squares
Square 57

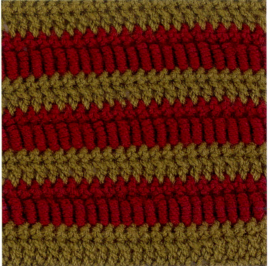

Colours A and B are required for this pattern.

With col A make 27 ch.

Row 1: (right side) cont with col A, tr (US dc) in 4th ch from hook and in each ch across—25 tr (US dc).

Row 2: cont with col A, 1 ch, turn, dc (US sc) in first st and in each st across to last 2 loops of last st, bringing in col B in last 2 loops to complete st, drop Col A—25 dc (US sc).

Row 3: cont with col B, 3 ch, turn, work bullion st in next st and in each st across to last st, tr (US dc) in last st—23 x bullion sts + 2 tr (US dc).

Row 4: cont with col B, repeat row 2, changing to col A—25 dc (US sc).

Row 5: cont with col A, 3 ch, turn, tr (US dc) in next and in each st across—25 tr (US dc).

Row 6: cont with col A, repeat row 2—25 dc (US sc).

Subsequent rows: repeat rows 3 to 6, ending with row 2, col A, finish off.

Bullion stitch: evenly wind yarn around hook 5 times, insert hook into next st and draw up a loop (even with height of bullion about to be made) and draw through all loops on hook until 2 loops remain, YO and draw through last 2 loops—bullion st made.

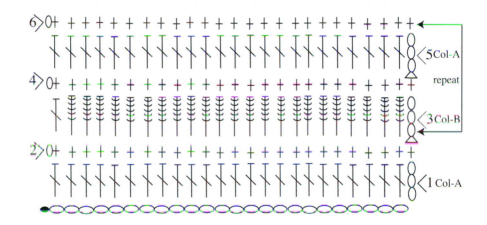

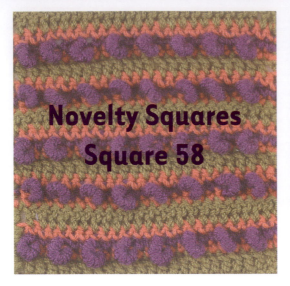

Colours A, C and D are required for this pattern.

With col A make 27 ch.

Row 1: (right side) cont with col A, tr (US dc) in 4th ch from hook and in each ch across, drop col A—25 tr (US dc).

Row 2: do not turn, remove hook and join col C with dc (US sc) in top of beginning ch at beginning of same row, dc (US sc) in next st and in each st across, drop col C—25 dc (US sc).

Row 3: do not turn, remove hook and join col D with dc (US sc) in first st of same row, dc (US sc) in next st, *work bent bullion st, dc (US sc) in next st, repeat from * across to last 2 loops of last st, bringing in col C in last 2 loops to complete st, finish off col D—8 x bent bullion sts.

Row 4: cont with col C, 1 ch, dc (US sc) in first and in each st across, drop col C—25 dc (US sc).

Row 5: do not turn, remove hook, reinsert in first st of same row and bring in col A, 3 ch, tr (US dc) in next st and in each st across, bringing in col C in last 2 loops of last st to complete st, drop col A—25 tr (US dc).

Row 6: cont with Col C, repeat row 4—25 dc (US sc).

Row 7: repeat row 3—8 x bent bullion sts.

Joining with dc (US sc): begin with a slip knot on hook. Insert hook into stitch or space indicated, YO and pull up loop, YO and draw through both loops on hook.

Row 8: cont with col C, repeat row 4, bringing in Col A in last 2 loops of last st to complete st, drop col C—25 dc (US sc).

Row 9: cont with col A, 3 ch, turn, tr (US dc) in next st and in each st across, drop col A—25 tr (US dc).

Subsequent rows: repeat from row 2, changing colour and turning work as required, finishing off with row 4 each time.

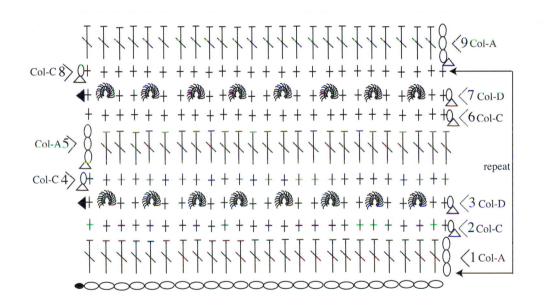 **Bent bullion stitch:** evenly wind yarn around hook 15 times, insert hook into next st and draw up a loop (even with height of bullion about to be made) and draw through all loops on hook until 2 loops remain, YO and draw through last 2 loops, dc (US sc) in next st—bent bullion st made.

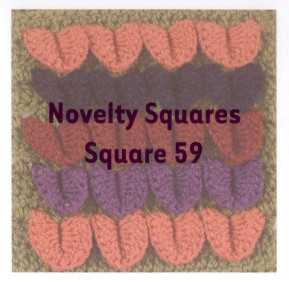

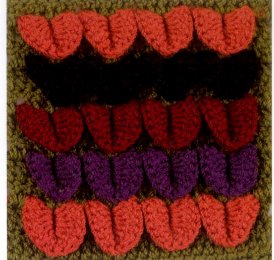

Colours A, B, C, D and E are required for this pattern.

With col A make 27 ch.

Row 1: cont with col A, tr (US dc) in 4th ch from hook and in each ch across—25 tr (US dc).

Row 2: (right side) cont with col A, 3 ch (count as tr [US dc]), turn, tr (US dc) in next and in each st across, drop col A—25 tr (US dc).

Row 3: do not turn, remove hook and join col C with ss in 3rd st at beginning of same row, *skip next st, work medallion st over next 2 sts, skip next st, ss in next st, repeat from * across, leave last 2 sts unused, finish off col C—4 x medallion sts.

Row 4: do not turn, remove hook, reinsert into last st of previous row and bring in Col A, 3 ch, turn, tr (US dc) in next st and in each st across—25 tr (US dc).

Row 5: cont with col A, repeat row 4, drop col A—25 tr (US dc).

Subsequent rows: repeat rows 3 to 5, alternating colours in the sequence A-C-A-D-A-B-A-E-A-C-A and turning work as required, ending with row 4, col A.

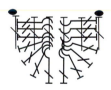

Medallion stitch: ss in st indicated, work 7 tr (US dc) around post of st indicated and 7 tr (US dc) around next st indicated, ss in st indicated—medallion st made.

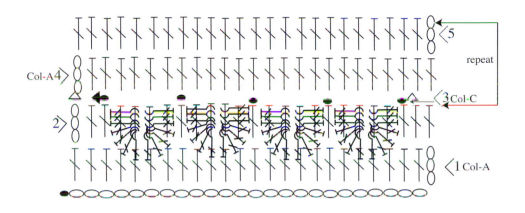

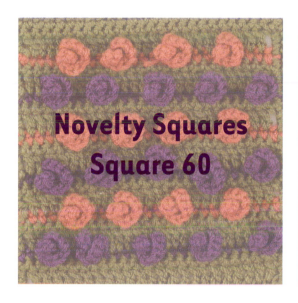

Novelty Squares
Square 60

Colours A, C and D are required for this pattern.

With col A make 27 ch.

Row 1: (right side) cont with col A, tr (US dc) in 4th ch from hook and in each ch across—25 tr (US dc).

Row 2: cont with col A, 1 ch, turn, dc (US sc) in first st and in each st across to last 2 loops of last st, bringing in col D

in last 2 loops to complete st, drop col A—25 dc (US sc).

Row 3: cont with col D, 1 ch, turn, dc (US sc) in first 2 sts, *work spiral, dc (US sc) in next 5 sts, repeat from * across to last 3 sts, dc (US sc) in each last 3 sts, finish off col D—5 x spirals.

Row 4: do not turn, remove hook, reinsert in first st of same row and bring in col A, 3 ch (count as tr [US dc]), working behind spirals tr (US dc) in next and in each st across—25 tr (US dc).

Row 5: cont with col A, repeat row 2, changing to col C—25 dc (US sc).

Row 6: cont with col C, 1 ch, turn, dc (US sc) in first 5 sts, *work spiral, dc (US sc) in next 5 sts, repeat from * across, finish off col C—4 x spirals.

Subsequent rows: repeat rows 3 to 6, ending with row 5, col A, finish off.

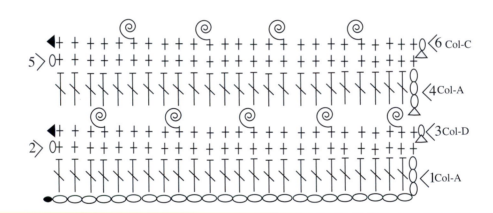 **Spiral:** working off dc (US sc) just made, make 5 ch, then work 3 dc (US sc) in 2nd ch from hook and 3 dc (US sc) in each next 3 ch, ss to dc (US sc) on working row—spiral made.

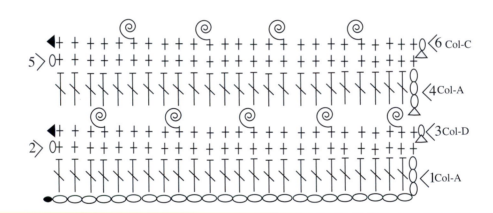

BRICKS AND BOXES

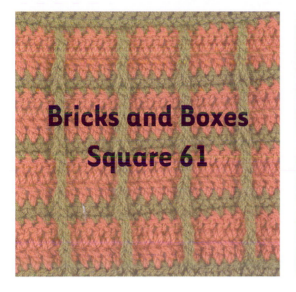

Bricks and Boxes
Square 61

Colours A and C are required for this pattern.

With col A make 26 ch.

Row 1: cont with col A, htr (US hdc) in 3rd ch from hook and in each ch across to last 3 loops of last st, bring in col C in last 3 loops to complete st, drop col A—25 htr (US hdc).

Row 2: (right side) cont with col C, 3 ch (count as tr [US dc]), turn, tr (US dc) in next st and in each st across—25tr (US dc).

Row 3: cont col C, repeat row 2, bringing in col A in last 2 loops of last st to complete st, drop col C—25tr (US dc).

Row 4: (skip unused st behind FPTtr [US dtr]) cont col A, 1 ch, turn, dc (US sc) in first 4 sts, *FPTtr (US dtr) around post of next st directly 3 rows below, dc (US sc) in next 4 sts, repeat from * across, dc (US sc) in last st—25 sts.

Row 5: cont col A, 1 ch, turn, dc (US sc) in first and in each st across, to last 2 loops of last st bringing in col C in last 2 loops to complete st, drop col A—25 sts.

Rows 6 and 7: repeat rows 2 and 3.

Row 8: cont col A, 1 ch, turn, dc (US sc) in first 4 sts, *FPTtr (US dtr) around post of next FPTtr (US dtr) directly 4 rows below, dc (US sc) in next 4 sts, repeat from * across, dc (US sc) in last st—25 sts.

Row 9: repeat row 5.

Rows 10 and 11: repeat rows 2 and 3.

Subsequent rows: repeat rows 4 to 9, ending with row 5, col A, finish off.

Front post triple treble (US front post double treble): YO 3 times, insert hook from front to back around post of st indicated, (YO and draw up a loop, YO and draw through 2 loops) 4 times—FPTtr (US FPdtr) made.

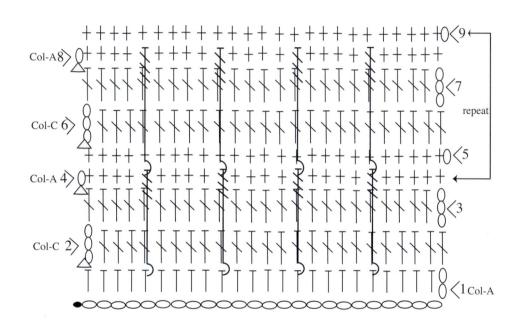

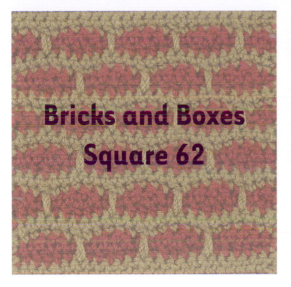

**Bricks and Boxes
Square 62**

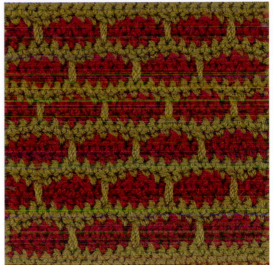

Colours A and B are required for this pattern.

With col A make 26 ch.

Row 1: cont with col A, dc (US sc) in 2nd ch from hook and in each ch across to last 2 loops of last st, bringing in col B in last 2 loops to complete st, drop col A—25 dc (US sc).

Row 2: (right side) cont with col B, 1 ch, turn, dc (US sc) in first 2 sts, *htr (US hdc) in next st, tr (US dc) in next st, htr (US hdc) in next st, dc (US sc) in next st, 1 ch, skip next st, dc (US sc) in next st, repeat from * across, dc (US sc) in last st—22 sts + 3 x 1-ch sps.

Row 3: cont with col B, repeat row 2 across to last 2 loops of last st, bringing in col A in last 2 loops to complete st, drop col B—25 sts.

Row 4: cont col A, 1 ch, turn, dc (US sc) in first 6 sts, *work Ltr (US Ldc) in skipped st 3 rows below, dc (US sc) in next 5 sts, repeat from * across, dc (US sc) in last st—3 x Ltr (US Ldc) + 22 dc (US sc).

Row 5: cont with col A, 1 ch, turn, dc (US sc) in first st and in each st across to last 2 loops of last st, bringing in col B in last 2 loops to complete st, drop col A—25 dc (US sc).

Row 6: cont with col B, 3 ch [count as tr (US dc)], htr (US hdc) in next st, *dc (US sc) in next st, 1 ch, skip next st, dc (US sc) in next st, htr (US hdc) in next st, tr (US dc) in next st, htr (US hdc) in next st, repeat from * across—25 sts.

Row 7: cont with col B, repeat row 6, changing to col A.

Row 8: cont with col A, 1 ch, turn, dc (US sc) in first 3 sts, *work Ltr (US Ldc) in skipped st 3 rows below, dc (US sc) in next 5 sts, repeat from * across, dc (US sc) in last 3 sts—4 x Ltr (US Ldc) + 21 dc (US sc).

Row 9: cont with col A, repeat row 5.

Subsequent rows: repeat rows 2 to 9, ending with row 5, col A.

Long treble (US long double crochet): YO, insert hook in st indicated, YO and pull up a loop even with st on working row, (YO and draw through 2 loops on hook) twice—Ltr (US Ldc) made.

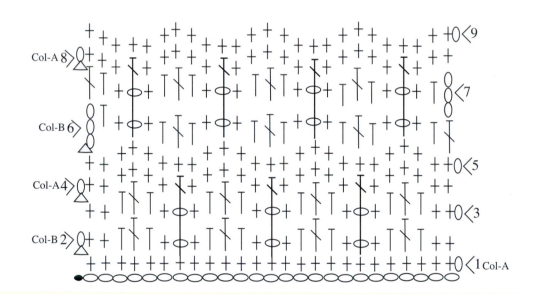

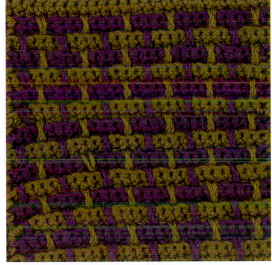

Colours A and D are required for this pattern.

With col A make 26 ch.

Row 1: (right side) cont with col A, dc (US sc) in 2nd ch from hook and in each ch across—25 dc (US sc).

Row 2: cont with col A, 1 ch, turn, dc (US sc) in first and in each st across to last 2 loops of last st, bringing in col D in last 2 loops to complete st, drop col A—25 dc (US sc).

Row 3: cont with col D, 1 ch, turn, working in back loops only, dc (US sc) in first 3 sts, *Ldc (US Lsc) in next st directly 2 rows below, dc (US sc) in next 3 sts, repeat from * across, dc (US sc) in last st—6 x Ldc (US Lsc).

Row 4: cont with col D, working in both loops, repeat row 2, changing to col

A—25 dc (US sc).

Row 5: cont with col A, 1 ch, turn, working in back loops only, dc (US sc) in first st, *Ldc (US Lsc) in next st directly 2 rows below, dc (US sc) in next 3 sts, repeat from * across—6 x Ldc (US Lsc).

Row 6: cont with col A, working in both loops, repeat row 2, changing to col D—25 dc (US sc).

Subsequent rows: repeat rows 3 to 6, ending with row 2, col A.

Long double crochet (US long single crochet): insert hook into stitch indicated and draw up a long loop level with stitch on working row, YO and draw through 2 loops on hook—Ldc (US Lsc) made.

✝ Work in back loops.

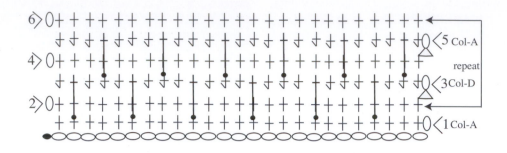

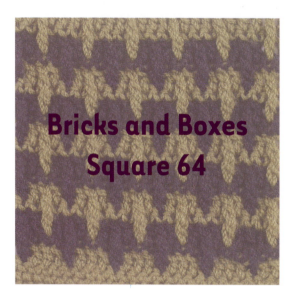

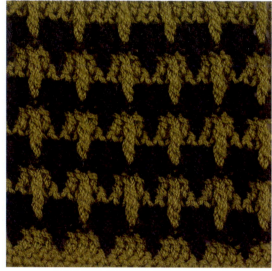

Bricks and Boxes
Square 64

Colours A and E are required for this pattern.

With col A make 26 ch.

Row 1: (right side) cont with col A, dc (US sc) in 2nd ch from hook and in each ch—25 dc (US sc).

Row 2: cont with col A, 3 ch (count as tr [US dc]), turn, tr (US dc) in next 2 st, 1 ch, skip next st, *tr (US dc) in next 3 sts, 1 ch, skip next st, repeat from * across to last st, tr (US dc) in last st, bringing in

col E in last 2 loops to complete st, drop col A—6 x 1-ch sps.

Row 3: cont with col E, 1 ch, turn, dc (US sc) in same st, *1 ch, skip next 1-ch sp, dc (US sc) in next 3 sts, repeat from * across—6 x 1-ch sps.

Row 4: cont col E, 4 ch (count as tr [US dc] + 1 ch), turn, *skip next st, tr (US dc) in next st, working in front of both 1-ch sps below, work dtr (US tr) in skipped st 4 rows below, tr (US dc) in next st, 1 ch, repeat from * across to last 2 loops of last st, bringing in col A in last 2 loops to complete st, drop col E—6 x 1-ch sps + 6 dtr (US tr).

Row 5: cont col A, 1 ch, turn, dc (US sc) in first 3 sts, *1 ch, skip next 1-ch sp, dc (US sc) in next 3 sts, repeat from * across to beginning 4-ch, 1 ch, dc (US sc) in 3rd ch of beginning 4-ch—6 x 1-ch sps.

Row 6: cont col A, 3 ch, turn, *working in front of both 1-ch sps below, work dtr (US tr) in skipped st 4 rows below, tr (US dc) in next st, 1 ch, skip next st, tr (US dc) in next st, repeat from * across to

last 2 sts, 1 ch, skip next st, tr (US dc) in last st, bringing in col E in last 2 loops of last st to complete st, drop col A—6 x 1-ch sps + 6 dtr (US tr).

Subsequent rows: repeat rows 3 to 6, ending with row 5, col A, and a last row as follows.

Last row: cont with col A, 3 ch, turn, *working in front of 1-ch sp below, work dtr (US tr) in skipped st 3 rows below, tr (US dc) in next 3 sts, repeat from * across—25 sts.

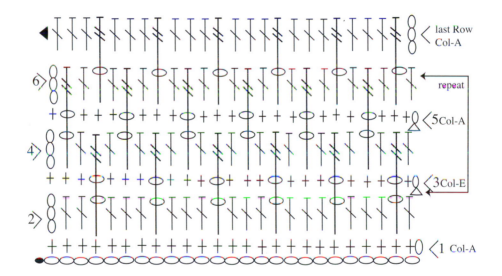

CHECK LIST

Basic stripes
- ☐ No 1
- ☐ No 2
- ☐ No 3
- ☐ No 4
- ☐ No 5

Spikes
- ☐ No 6
- ☐ No 7
- ☐ No 8
- ☐ No 9
- ☐ No 10

Shells
- ☐ No 11
- ☐ No 12
- ☐ No 13
- ☐ No 14
- ☐ No 15

Zigzags
- ☐ No 16

- ☐ No 17
- ☐ No 18
- ☐ No 19
- ☐ No 20

Reliefs
- ☐ No 21
- ☐ No 22
- ☐ No 23
- ☐ No 24
- ☐ No 25

Ripples
- ☐ No 26
- ☐ No 27
- ☐ No 28
- ☐ No 29
- ☐ No 30

Chains
- ☐ No 31
- ☐ No 32
- ☐ No 33

- ☐ No 34
- ☐ No 35

Mosaics
- ☐ No 36
- ☐ No 37
- ☐ No 38
- ☐ No 39
- ☐ No 40

Clusters and bobbles
- ☐ No 41
- ☐ No 42
- ☐ No 43
- ☐ No 44
- ☐ No 45

Afghans
- ☐ No 46
- ☐ No 47
- ☐ No 48
- ☐ No 49

- ☐ No 50

Variable stripes
- ☐ No 51
- ☐ No 52
- ☐ No 53
- ☐ No 54
- ☐ No 55

Novelties
- ☐ No 56
- ☐ No 57
- ☐ No 58
- ☐ No 59
- ☐ No 60

Bricks and boxes
- ☐ No 61
- ☐ No 62
- ☐ No 63
- ☐ No 64

CHECK LIST

Basic stripes
- ☐ No 1
- ☐ No 2
- ☐ No 3
- ☐ No 4
- ☐ No 5

Spikes
- ☐ No 6
- ☐ No 7
- ☐ No 8
- ☐ No 9
- ☐ No 10

Shells
- ☐ No 11
- ☐ No 12
- ☐ No 13
- ☐ No 14
- ☐ No 15

Zigzags
- ☐ No 16

- ☐ No 17
- ☐ No 18
- ☐ No 19
- ☐ No 20

Reliefs
- ☐ No 21
- ☐ No 22
- ☐ No 23
- ☐ No 24
- ☐ No 25

Ripples
- ☐ No 26
- ☐ No 27
- ☐ No 28
- ☐ No 29
- ☐ No 30

Chains
- ☐ No 31
- ☐ No 32
- ☐ No 33

- ☐ No 34
- ☐ No 35

Mosaics
- ☐ No 36
- ☐ No 37
- ☐ No 38
- ☐ No 39
- ☐ No 40

Clusters and bobbles
- ☐ No 41
- ☐ No 42
- ☐ No 43
- ☐ No 44
- ☐ No 45

Afghans
- ☐ No 46
- ☐ No 47
- ☐ No 48
- ☐ No 49

- ☐ No 50

Variable stripes
- ☐ No 51
- ☐ No 52
- ☐ No 53
- ☐ No 54
- ☐ No 55

Novelties
- ☐ No 56
- ☐ No 57
- ☐ No 58
- ☐ No 59
- ☐ No 60

Bricks and boxes
- ☐ No 61
- ☐ No 62
- ☐ No 63
- ☐ No 64

SUPPLIER

Bendigo Woollen Mills

4 Lansell Street

Bendigo Vic. 3550

ph: 03 5442 4600

fax: 03 5442 2918

www.bendigowoollenmills.com.au